Truth and Lies
in Architecture

ORO Editions
Publishers of Architecture, Art, and Design
Gordon Goff: Publisher

www.oroeditions.com
info@oroeditions.com

Published by ORO Editions

Copyright © 2022 Richard Francis-Jones

Author: Richard Francis-Jones
Book Design: Alicia McCarthy
Project Manager: Jake Anderson

10 9 8 7 6 5 4 3 2 1 First Edition

ISBN: 978-1-954081-65-9

Color Separations and Printing: ORO Group Ltd.
Printed in China.

ORO Editions makes a continuous effort to minimize the overall carbon
footprint of its publications. As part of this goal, ORO Editions, in association
with Global ReLeaf, arranges to plant trees to replace those used in the manufac-
turing of the paper produced for its books. Global ReLeaf is an international
campaign run by American Forests, one of the world's oldest nonprofit
conservation organizations. Global ReLeaf is American Forests' education and
action program that helps individuals, organizations, agencies, and corporations
improve the local and global environment by planting and caring for trees.

Truth and Lies
in Architecture

Richard Francis-Jones
Foreword by Kenneth Frampton

For Lina

Contents

Foreword

Kenneth Frampton

Written by a leading Australian architect these essays represent a level of critical awareness rarely found within the architectural profession and one would be hard pressed to find another comparable figure in contemporary architectural practice.

It is significant that the first essay in this collection should be devoted to the theme of melancholy, a frame of mind to which architects are particularly prone due to the multiple environmental conditions that confront us at this particular moment in history. As Francis-Jones puts it:

Today is surely not the time for the loud, over-confidence of dominating master architects, those times and what they achieved, good or bad, have passed. The challenges we now face seem to require the pensiveness and sensitivity of melancholy...The melancholy of the architect may be the only true and authentic 'place' from which we can begin to work with the vexed conditions of contemporary life. The architect can start here. Perhaps this is the shore from which our projects can be launched.

Written over the last two decades, the essays reflect on the difficulty of practicing architecture in the first quarter of the twenty-first century. To this end they are as much about the aporia of contemporary society as they are addressed to the difficulty of achieving an ethical and liberative environmental culture in our time. With regard to this last, Francis-Jones finds himself opposed to the various ways in which the profession has attempted to establish its legitimacy in an age dominated by the values of techno-scientific instrumentality. These are the various evasive stratagems by which the profession has presented itself over the past half century as it has oscillated between masquerading as a metier akin to applied science or at another moment as a language or yet again as an abstract culture similar to music or eventually as little more than a 'decorated shed.' This last would lead the profession to justify itself by way of branding; as being responsible for designing buildings as if they were primarily spectacular pieces of gigantic sculpture.

At the same time, the author remains acutely aware that neither critical reflection nor architectural theory are capable of assisting in directly applicable to the arcane process by which one arrives at a parti from which an architecture of quality may evolve by way of an informed intuition predicated on the interplay between site, program, budget, durability and the escalating impact of a changing climate.

In this regard, the author reminds us that, as opposed to our increasingly techno-scientific division of labor, architects are confronted with the direct constraints of contemporary reality on a daily basis, in which, amongst other challenges, they have to reconcile the increasingly challenging demands of real estate speculation with the increasingly bureaucratic complexity of contemporary building regulations. It is just this habitual, hyper-awareness that makes architects particularly susceptible to the aporetic conditions that prevail in contemporary society. Hence, in an essay entitled, 'The Truth of Architecture and the Lies of Architecture', we read of "...the insidious process that displaced all human values: The parasitic meta-ideology of commodification, an all-consuming valuelessness through which we are reduced from citizens to mere consumers." Later on in much the same vein we encounter the author's assertion that: "...alienation no longer bothers us. We accept and indulge in our isolation...only the most extreme acts of human violence and environmental vandalism will momentarily disturb us from our flotation." Elsewhere we encounter a similar fatalistic awareness when he writes:

We are overwhelmed with information, more than we can possibly deal with, to the extent that it rolls over us with no time to distinguish between facts, opinions, and deceptions...we have become data junkies unable to distinguish the laboring of life from the laboring of home-life.

One of the most enlightening essays in this anthology is a piece entitled, '*The Slowness of Architecture and the Speed of the Architect*', wherein the author reflects on the double-blind attending contemporary building when he writes:

11

Building processes themselves have actually changed very little, they are not significantly quicker but the speed and volume of information surrounding the production have increased exponentially. Projects are now developed in a sea of information, more and more information is required to build a building. ...But is the work much better and is it quicker, or more compromised, more wasteful?

Elsewhere Francis-Jones links this informatic overload to the universal condition of homelessness, both literally and psycho-sociologically. He concludes, somewhat surprisingly with the words:

Therefore the silent architecture of Mies van der Rohe can perhaps escape ideology and mystification through a seeming indifference to dwelling, a deeply poetic testament to its absence. Developing from this, a contemporary architecture that reflects the impossibility of dwelling can succeed in obtaining a form of authenticity. The Farnsworth House in Illinois constructed shortly before the Seagram Building in 1951 is a clear acknowledgement of our non-dwelling. Within the Farnsworth House, 'liberated' humanity is suspended from the world in which it can no longer dwell. The sparse and purified platforms permit no masks of comforting self-deception but instead confront us with the reality of our estrangement. While the natural is preserved only through emphatic separation from our corrupting presence.

In contrast, Francis-Jones cites Jørn Utzon's first house in Porto Petro, Mallorca and remarks that here, albeit momentarily, is found a place to dwell that, as he puts it, "...does not violate the site because it is the site." At the same time he perceptively observes, "It has a primordial quality but lies within the project of modernity." It is ironic that this 'home coming' should involve a Danish architect building a vacation house for himself on a remote cliff-top site, sequestered in the Balearic Islands.

This critical tone is complimented throughout by Francis-Jones's didactic illustrations for this is an architect who, throughout his career, has not only been affected by the iconographic culture of painting, photography and film, but also by two antithetical but complimentary philosophical traditions, that is by existential phenomenology in the first instance and by Marxist critical theory in the second, this last being confirmed by his citation of Fredric Jameson. At the same time the author draws our attention to the largely uninhabitable expanse of Australia through two unforgettable aerial images of the continent as an infinite desert, first, a dramatic aerial shot of the 3,488 mile 'dingo fence' crossing in a straight line over the empty land mass and second, a similar shot of Uluru, formerly known as Ayres' Rock, as seen from an even greater height in Kata Tjuta National Park. Both images forcibly remind us of the continent's Aboriginal population. It is to this end that he includes an image of Glenn Murcutt's masterly Marika Alderton beach house, completed in Yirrkala in the Northern Territory in 1994. Here, despite the fact that the architect has made a great effort to respect the domestic mores of Aboriginal life, the aura of an ineluctable homelessness remains.

Acknowledgement
of Country

1 Mahon Pool, Maroubra, part of
the coastal land south of Sydney for
which the Bidjigal and Gadigal people
are traditional custodians.

This series of texts was written in Maroubra, a diverse beachside suburb on the south-east coast of Sydney.

The name 'Maroubra' may derive from the Dharug word 'murab-ara', 'loud-noise-having' or 'like thunder'[1] referring perhaps to the loudness of the surf crashing against the rocks which characterise the rugged landscape. It is a beautiful and dramatic meeting of water and land, a long beach and framed by windswept peninsulas. In the rock carvings at the northern headland, there is evidence of the presence of the Muru-ora-dial Aboriginal people, who camped and fished at Maroubra many years ago.

The Bidjigal and Gadigal people are the traditional custodians of this coastal land of Sydney which includes Maroubra, and I acknowledge their custodianship of this land and waters and pay my respects to their Elders past, present and emerging.

Over the last two hundred and thirty years Aboriginal and Torres Strait Islander peoples have been systematically dispossessed, disempowered and marginalised. European occupation and settlement imposed a modern conception of land and animal life purely in instrumental terms of possession, ownership and exploration. Lost has been the concept of custodianship and a human interconnectedness with the land. Deep pre-modern cultural knowledge has been systematically and fatally undermined, overridden, or worse commodified.

An acknowledgement of country represents deference to the deep histories of this place that are beyond our modern understanding. It is an acknowledgement of the injustices and oppression that has been suffered upon First Nations people in Australia. It is an acknowledgement and deference of respect and regret for social, cultural and environmental damage, pain and destruction beyond repair.

1 Jeremy Steele, *Morooberra, the person, and Maroubra, the place, Sydney Aboriginal Language Insights* <http://naabawinya.blogspot.com/2011/05/morooberra-person-and-maroubra-place.html>, 2011.

2 Australian Bureau of Statistics, *Prisoners in Australia*, 2020.

However, such acknowledgements must seem a little thin or even veiling at a time when the injustice, suffering and destruction is continuing.

Aboriginal and Torres Strait Islander people make up just over three percent of the population of Australia yet last year made up twenty-nine percent of its prison population[2] a ratio that does not appear to be diminishing. Last year also witnessed the destruction for mining exploration of the caves in Juukan Gorge, Western Australia, a sacred site for the traditional owners of the land, the Puutu Kunti Kurrama and Pinikura peoples. The cave was the only inland site in Australia to show signs of continuous human occupation for over forty-six thousand years.

Aboriginal and Torres Strait Islander people should be aware that this publication may contain images or names of deceased persons in photographs and printed material that some people may find distressing.

Introduction

Architecture has never been more challenged than it is today. Addressing the sheer scale of the triple challenges of environmental sustainability, in the form of climate change; the social, in the form of class, gender and racial inequality; and the cultural, in terms of identity, exclusion and prejudice in particular against First Nations People, is a seemingly overwhelmingly task for architecture.

At the same time these great challenges come at a moment when architecture has never been so marginalised and diminished. The practice of architecture has been progressively desiccated, undermined and commodified through the instrumental processes of the contemporary development industry and professional practice, together with the simplistic reductionism of media technology and market consumption demand.

How could this happen? How can the true nature of architecture have been so undermined?

This collection of short essays is a series of explorations and excavations into this vexed territory in an attempt to uncover the depth and nature of the diminishment of contemporary architecture and the tracks that lead us here.

I have come to believe that the whole world is an enigma, a harmless enigma that is made terrible by our own mad attempt to interpret it as though it had an underlying truth.

Umberto Eco, *Foucault's Pendulum* (1988) [1]

One can sometimes see more clearly in a person who is lying than in one who is telling the truth. Like light, truth dazzles. Untruth, on the other hand, is a beautiful dusk that enhances everything.

Albert Camus, *The Fall* (1956) [2]

[1] Umberto Eco, translated by William Weaver, *Foucault's Pendulum,* New York: A Helen and Kurt Wolff Book/ Harcourt Brace Jovanovich.

[2] Albert Camus, translated from the original *La Chute* by Justin O'Brien, *The Fall*, UK: Penguin, 2006.

Prologue:
Melancholy
of the Architect

Melancholy is sadness that has taken on lightness.

Italo Calvino, *Lightness* (1988) [1]

1 Italo Calvino, '*Lightness*', *Six Memos for the Next Millennium*, Harvard University Press, 1988.

2 Tony Toscani, *Daydreamer*, 2018.

Overwhelmed

It is difficult to think deeply about architecture, without a kind of sadness born of the relation between the magnitude of the task and the relative helplessness of the architect.

The gravity of the task seems overwhelming for the architecture of our time: The looming environmental catastrophe of climate change and species extinction; the injustice, and cruelty of socially and politically embedded inequity, prejudice, and oppression; the reduction of our work to image, to a commodity; and our own cultural alienation and disconnection from an authentic relationship with the place where we build, and indeed each other.

We only manage to cope, it seems, through the distractions of hyper-consumption, media information technology that feeds our own individual truths, and the noisy illusion of marginal democratic participation.

If we do stop for a moment and reflect on the work of the architect within this vortex of distress, self-obsession and distraction, then we may conclude that we are really just part of the problem. If we knock down an existing building and re-build a new 'sustainable' highly performing one, then still it will take many years, before we offset the relative embodied carbon cost of the new build. If we start with an unbuilt site, then what cost is the loss of green-footprint, damage to the landscape, or indeed the flattening effect on the specificity and identity of place that usually results.

In any event, we are all usually too overwhelmed by the proliferation of images driving an incessant updating of self-conscious architectural fashion that demands a seemingly senseless rate of energy consumption and carbon generation, to even notice.

We might, with some justification, think that we are indeed part of the problem and the best thing we can do is stop—stop these new buildings, stop the production of beguiling new images, and take a break, go on sabbatical maybe.

But we are trapped, we cannot stop nor turn back. The processes of growth and the rapid and intense rate of urbanisation are unstoppable. This is not going to stop for the architect to reconsider the direction of our work and industry let alone try to turn its course; it is well beyond our control.

No wonder, when the architect pauses, turns off the phone, silences the alerts that remind us we are behind, overdue and out of date, then turns off all the tablets and screens that stream constant entertainment and distraction...
After a moment of peace.
It is a mist of melancholy that descends.

What is this sense of sadness, where does it come from? Is it simply a rational reaction to the impossibility of the task or is it something in the nature of the architect, maybe something in our training or professional culture?

Negativity

There is a duality to the culture of architecture and the training of the architect. Perhaps it is born of the inherent duality of our work positioned between science and art, between the measurable and the immeasurable, function and form, practice and theory, and perhaps most relevant between optimism and pessimism, the positive and the negative.

To project into the future a vision that binds people together to the extent that aspirations can be realised, notwithstanding the great threats and challenges of the processes of construction, requires positive belief and real optimism.

Approval processes, client and stakeholder consultation, technical challenges and limitations, time and cost pressures, all will threaten to compromise and dilute the vision of the project. The architect must be the champion of the project, ready to listen and understand, and constantly look to improve and refine rather than compromise. Above all, the architect must believe these hurdles can be overcome, spread the belief that something good and noble can be achieved.

Architects are then by necessity and nature positive, supportive and optimistic.

But there seems to be a flip side to the character of the architect.

Architects are also pretty negative, particularly in relation to each other. We are hard on our professional colleagues, quick to criticise and denigrate, and generally keen to focus on the faults and weaknesses.

Is it because we have just exhausted our positivity through the constant projection of optimism that our work demands? Is there some kind of inevitable rebalancing of Yang to an overplayed Yin?

Or is it the brutality of our industry that has done this to us? Is it because we have been somehow so traumatised by the stress and pressures in our professional lives that we have developed a paranoid and distorted view of our colleagues, when the real threats are elsewhere?

More likely, it is born of our training and in particular the predominance of the negative critique in our schools of architecture. The negative critique seems to be a foundation of the education of the architect, reaching a focus in the 'jury' criticism of major projects often with external 'jurors', where the student is expected to present and then 'defend' the proposition. The language seems needlessly negative and combative, more suited to the courtroom setting and trial of an accused. What qualities does this process reward and engender in the student of architecture?

How much creative talent, sensitivity and potential is rejected and crushed? Why is there not a more nurturing, supportive and encouraging culture of learning? Is it because of a simple-minded and self-perpetuating view that it is very tough in this industry, and you better toughen up?

The extent of this professional culture of negativity is a burden for the architect. But equally challenging for the architect and any would-be agent of creative change, innovation and optimism, is the more all-pervasive human bias towards negativity.

2 Amrisha Vaish, Tobias Grossmann, Amanda Woodward, *Not all emotions are created equal: the negativity bias in social-emotional development*, Psychological Bulletin Vol. 134, No. 3, pp.383-403, American Psychological Association, 2008.

This is the imbalance or asymmetry in the way we attend to and focus on negative rather than positive information and events in our world. Supported through a broad range of psychological research[2] it seems clear that from early childhood we bias the negative, it focuses our attention, will mark our memory, and figure in our thinking and actions notably more than the positive, which is all too easily overlooked and obscured. While there would seem to be an understandable evolutionary rationale to such prioritising, in our contemporary lives and challenges, such negative prioritising makes less sense. In many ways this bias works against our interest, it is shaping our perspectives and action with inaccuracy. The negative is a magnet for our attention, hence, for example, the asymmetry in our news and media, and this negative imbalance is only intensifying through contemporary information technology and social media.

Our professional culture and the natural human bias seem to result in two different responses from the architect. A kind of reactionary embrace, characterised by an overconfident and righteous self-belief, empowered through an opposition or competing negativity and intensified in the wake of success. Or a deeper realisation and understanding, perhaps intuitive, of the nature of the task, its complexity and vastness in relation to our trivial self-reference, that engenders a profound sense of melancholy.

Melancholia

Melancholy is beyond the dichotomy between the positive and negative, it is a state of recognition and acknowledgement of the human struggle with the way of the world or more accurately, our way with the world. It is at neither of the poles of optimism nor pessimism, but in today's circumstances, it can only truly be an experience of some sadness. Generally, we think of melancholia as synonymous with depression; a debilitating mental health disorder of persistent sadness and demotivation to be treated with medication to correct the chemical imbalance that is giving us a distorted perception of the world and our place in it.

3 G. Vasari, *Le vite de'più eccellenti pittori, scultori ed architettori nelle redazioni del 1550 e 1558*, ed. R. Bettarini & P. Barocchi, 6 vols. IV: 439, (Florence: Sansoni, 1966-87), quoted from, Piers D. G. Britton, *Raphael and the bad humours of painters in Vasari's "Lives of the Artists"* Renaissance Studies, April 2008, Vol. 22, No. 2 (April 2008), pp. 187 Published by: Wiley, https://www.jstor.org/stable/24417236.

People with this condition generally slow right down, slow their movements, slow their speech, and perhaps even thoughts. They withdraw from a world that seems to have no place for them, a world deaf to their silence.

If we hold back the beguiling intensity and distractions of contemporary life, this sense of melancholia may seem a natural and inevitable reaction to our modern alienation, disconnection, and placelessness. Where grasping for slowness and silence may make sense and even hold some promise of truth.

This is perhaps closer to what we know as the artistic sense of melancholia expressed by writers and artists from the early modern period. In the sixteenth century, the work of Giorgio Vasari suggested that a special artistic insight and achievement is gained through this state of mind.

We often see that in the exercise of letters and of the intellectual-cum-manual arts, those who are melancholic are more assiduous in their studies and support with the greater patience the weight of their labours; and hence it is rare for those of this humour not to achieve excellence...[3]

Beginning perhaps with Albrecht Dürer's famous allegorical woodcut *Melencolia I* (1514), artists, through to our modern period, have represented this state of melancholy as a pensive figure, despondent and sober, head in hands, thoughtful and lost.

But no matter the artist, each of these figures of melancholy has a penetrating gaze, is looking out into the middle distance, is searching for a way through the malaise.

Perhaps melancholia is a necessary ingredient to a creative act of any depth. Perhaps artistic truth of consequence must be born out of sadness and doubt, born from reflection and thoughtfulness, from slowness, and a withdrawal of the self.

Today is surely not the time for the loud overconfidence of dominating 'master' architects; those times and what they delivered, good and bad, have passed.

The complexity and nature of the challenges we now face seem to require the pensiveness and sensitivity of melancholy.

We are now less certain, more circumspect. We must know that mere appearance and images are not enough. All we have is the wisdom of doubt and melancholy, which ultimately might be worth more.

The melancholy of the architect may be the only true and authentic 'place' from which we can begin to work within the vexed conditions of contemporary life. The architect can start here. Perhaps this is the shore from which our projects can be launched.

3 Albrecht Dürer, *Melencolia I,* 1514.

The Theory
of Architecture
and the Intuition
of the Architect

4 Pablo Picasso, *La Nageuse*, 1929.

Practice

Contemporary architectural practice is far removed from the world of theory. In many ways, it is an antithetical world, of high-pressure intense material, action and reaction, where there is no time to consider the theoretical and cultural implications of our actions, no time for cerebral reflection.

Architectural practice is caught, well and truly, in the tide of the property development and construction industries. Sunk deep in the regulatory, financial, and procurement processes, politics and pragmatism that characterise this world. It can be hard to breathe or even survive in this tense and demanding environment, let alone develop and evolve our work in relation to the larger cultural issues of architectural theory. We are too overwhelmed at the sheer challenge of realising a project with some conceptual integrity, to simultaneously critique or even properly understand the nature of what we do.

So, within this world of pragmatism and practice, how does the architect thoughtfully respond to contemporary theoretical issues? How can the project of architecture have this essential dimension?

Theory

Architectural theory is a world away from practice. The critical insights of theory will offer little assistance to the architect drowning in the pressures and pragmatics of professional practice. In fact, theory is in many ways an impediment to practice. It is probably going to make it harder, like throwing a weight at a struggling swimmer. It is hardly surprising then, that most practicing architects have little time for theory as they struggle to just stay afloat.

This sea of practice is full of threatening currents of conflict, competing demands, complexity, urgency and accusation. It is deeply disorienting, and it can be difficult to know where you are heading, where is the shore and even, what is the point? Only when we stop for a moment and step out of the tide that we are trying to swim with or against, will we be able to look back at what it is we are doing and reflect on its nature. This critical reflection is vital to understanding the values, ethics and meaning behind the work, and how it influences the public good. We desperately need a moment out of the sea and a platform to rest on.

This is the space of theory; this is the space for which the architect yearns, a temporary respite on some form of critical platform of reflection. It may still bob around with the current, is not always so comfortable and in the end, will throw us back in, but without it, without this respite and reflection, we may lose our bearings completely and go under, taking the project of architecture with us.

This fragile platform of theory is the meeting place between the academy and the profession, a place of brief, momentary respite and reflection. All too soon we will have to jump back in or be washed off before we are ready. But hopefully, we will return to the currents of practice with improved insight, a renewed sense of direction and a determination to keep your heads above the sea.

Engagement

The greatest challenge for the architect in these very difficult waters, is the natural flow and tide of the development and construction industry, which is not towards architecture at all, but building, understood as an optimised investment object utilising standardised conventional construction techniques to maximising return and minimising cost. It is the pursuit of the most market-driven image with the least means and least substance. This is its natural course.

The planning and regulatory systems attempt to mediate this instrumental flow through the protection of the public realm, environment, and amenity. However, this is necessarily a defensive restrictive action and will therefore generally be inherently conservative and inhibit creative insight and paradigm change.

Perhaps the only way to really survive the flow and drag is to find shallower, safer waters in the form of sheltered supportive commissions or to understand exactly the ebb and flow, the tide and character such that we can move with it, while still clinging firmly to our renewed sense of theoretical insight, and in doing so, perhaps make small changes to the direction of the current itself.

But beyond such rare protective harbours and sheltered privileged commissions, how can the architect engage with the project of theory which seems so contradictory to the demanding pragmatics of practice, as even within such protective spaces, there remains the pressures and immediacies that overwhelm time for thought and reflection?

Intuition

It is perhaps through the avoidance of thought, through thoughtless action.

The drawing of the first line across the page intersects the site with the programme, simultaneously exploring, discovering, and uncovering the project that is, in some ways already there.

Thought and theory are ironically sometimes an impediment to understanding; at least the understanding that comes directly through action. Certainly, they are impediments to intuition, and intuition is perhaps the primary means through which the architect engages, via the architectural project, with the pressing cultural and theoretical issues of our time.

Intuition is an existential quality: it is beyond the rational. It is rooted in a deeper connection to the world we inhabit; it is our feeling, rather than our knowledge. It is a manifestation of the interconnectedness of all things. Remarkably, it is the means for a wholistic response to the vastly complex nature of our human condition.

It is a response that comes less from us, than through us.

But this first intuitive line, drawn across the site, this formal concept must be transformed, constructed, and assembled through technique and material to become architecture, and this will require direct engagement with the market and industry, with all its limitations, and possibilities.

So, following theoretical respite, the architect must jump back into the waters of practice, with eyes wide open, and find a way to improve our stroke.

The Truth of Architecture and the Lies of the Architect

Truth is like poetry and most people fucking hate poetry.

The Big Short (2015) [1]

1 'overheard at a Washington, DC, bar' quote that appears on screen midway through the film, written by Adam McKay, co-writer and director, *The Big Short*, 2015.

5 Donald Trump at a campaign rally
at the American Airlines Centre on
September 14, 2015 in Dallas, Texas.

Truth and Lies

The concept of 'truth' is a perennial and vexed issue for architecture.

Can architecture lay any claim to truth? Can architecture have a moral effect or purpose? Or is architecture indifferent to the intention of its makers and the actions it accommodates?

At this moment, when we are surrounded by so much noise, polarisation, argument and intolerance, questions of fact and accuracy, let alone truth are suppressed, obscured, buried, or most worrying, even irrelevant. We are now living and working as architects in the era of 'Post-Truth'.

The word *Post-Truth* was first used in 1992[2] but it is only in 2016, coincidentally the year of Donald Trump's election to the US presidency, that it has become commonplace and generally now understood to refer to the shaping of public opinion through emotive appeals to personal beliefs, rather than objective facts. These appeals have been enhanced and amplified through the dominance of social media, which tends to equalise source legitimacy. Volume and frequency of repetition have become key validations over measurable or scientific data. We seek views and opinions that reinforce our own, rather than search for something approaching the truth.

Post-Truth has now become a numbing and exhausting contagion within our political and community 'discourse', which for those not located at the extremes, engenders fatigue and apathy further alienating us from any real interest in truth.

Architecture is naturally infected with this bending and distortion of community and cultural discourse. But this is not the only distortion in any conceptual search for truth. Drawing on developments in digital effects in film making and gaming, image production in architecture has become highly advanced and ubiquitous in the consumption and even evaluation of architecture. It is through this digital lens that we now 'see' architecture.

2 According to Oxford Dictionaries, the first time the term post-truth was used was in a 1992 essay by the late Serbian-American playwright Steve Tesich in the Nation magazine. There is evidence of the phrase post-truth being used before Tesich's article, but apparently with the transparent meaning 'after the truth was known', and not with the new implication that truth itself has become irrelevant. The recent expansion in meaning of the prefix "post-", rather than simply referring to the time after a specified situation or event – as in post-war or post-match", in post-truth it had taken on the meaning of "belonging to a time in which the specified concept has become unimportant or irrelevant". The nuance, it said, originated in the mid-20th century, and has been used in formations such as post-national (1945) and post-racial (1971).

While the photographic image of architecture has been dominant throughout the twentieth-century, the fabricated digital image is now not only hegemonic but it has become difficult to distinguish between a photograph of a constructed building and the Computer Generated Image (CGI), so developed is the quality of digital image production.

Similar and related developments in material technology have produced a wide range of synthetic materials that overcome many of the 'performance' limitations of natural materials, improving durability, decay resistance, thermal movement, recycling, and waterproofness. But, more disturbingly, many of these synthetics have carefully engineered appearances that closely simulate natural materials. For example, a synthetic composite porcelain panel can now be almost impossible to distinguish in appearance from a slab of natural Carrara Marble.

These advances offer alternatives and opportunities for the composition and performance of our work, but they are also a little disorientating and there can be a certain feeling of loss, disconnection, and reduction to the materials and very nature of our work. At moments we may remember the modernist call for 'honesty' and 'truth to materials' and have a certain longing or nostalgia for a time of greater certainty when it seemed possible to talk more meaningfully about truth in architecture.

Truth

Modernism was a singular and focused project, an incisive instrument for dealing with our world, cutting cleanly through our social and environmental challenges with unquestioning confidence. The key instrument of this modernism was scientific knowledge. Through it, we were liberated from myth and religion for a 'true' and reliable path towards human emancipation and enlightenment. The knowledge was real, it was exciting and it delivered. We developed enormous capability and capacity for controlling our environment, our health and social evolution through technology and a scientific understanding of the natural world.

It gave certainty, direction, unity, and dazzling potential. It was progress, not just in terms of technical development and evolution but as a noun with a capital P. In 'Progress', we had something to believe in, a truth we could count on.

But it had a flip side, a blindness that became something of a betrayal of the enlightenment vision of the modern project. The singular truth of modernism and the march of 'Progress' became intolerant, with cultural and ethnic diversity, inclusion and equity trampled underfoot. Enabled through scientific and technological advancements the twentieth-century witnessed an unleashing of human suffering and environmental degradation on a breathtaking scale. It was a century of such astounding 'Progress' that it almost killed us all.

Architecture, likewise, intoxicated with the confidence of truth, played its part in this human and environmental degradation. European cities and towns were twice damaged, first through the violence of the second world war and then through post-war urban reconstruction. International modernism became hegemonic, flattening cultural differentiation and human connections to the land while undermining the environment and First Nations communities through ignorance and indifference. Architecture became primarily quantitative and measurable, a singular truth that ultimately left it robbed and soulless.

Beware those who claim to possess the truth. We were naive, the modernist truth was deeply ideological. Our connection with each other and with our world is infinitely more complex and culturally layered than the singularity of modernist truth.

But this late twentieth-century realisation came too late. We were already almost entirely displaced, alienated and disconnected from alternative earthly truths, while the fragmented and marginalised socio-cultures that still retained pre-modern knowledge were fatally damaged and dispossessed.

6 The Bijlmer modernist housing
estate near Amsterdam constructed
in 1966, provided 40,000 dwellings
predominantly in high rise geometric
linear forms.

Truths

The post-modernism of the late twentieth-century pushed back hard. Revealing the contingent and subjective nature of modern truth and the meta-narrative, uncovering its ideological and instrumental nature and promoting more critical, broader, inclusive and socially conditioned 'truths'. Architecture was released from the tight, abstract constraints of modernism, set free to rediscover its past, turn to its traditions and interdependence with a local culture of place.

But once alienated, is such a return possible or do we only further undermine, through our thin patronising ignorance, what we seek to reclaim?

Something else had happened also, something sinister that undermined this 'turn' and made it almost beside the point. Our noble project of knowledge and human emancipation enabled by scientific knowledge was Faustian and released something far more destructive than the power of our science and technology, a force that refuses to ever return to its Pandora's box and defies all attempts at control and mediation and is now too deep within us to ever leave.

Replacing myth, religion, ritual, continuity and interconnected knowledge was not just scientific knowledge but an insidious process that displaced all human values: The parasitic meta-ideology of commodification, an all-consuming valuelessness through which we are reduced from citizens to mere consumers. A seemingly harmless and useful process, growing like a disease, whereby gradually everything we touch is reduced to a commodity, slowly infected and erased of meaning. Everything is a commodity: every cultural movement, every art form and protest.

Every resistance is recuperated into a system of valueless, meaningless exchange that feeds on itself.

Enabled by our endlessly expanding technology now even our very identity we readily give up to commodification and, seemingly happily, collaborate in our own demise and disappearance.

7 A large billboard stands on top of a Nike store showing former San Francisco 49ers quarterback Colin Kaepernick at Union Square in San Francisco in 2018.

Social values themselves, progressive, good and maybe even true, are now able to be immediately processed and diluted for ready commodification. Think of the artful and highly crafted Nike Colin Kaepernick advertising campaign of 2018 or the Gillette 'Toxic Masculinity'campaign of 2019 that commodified progressive social values against oppressive social norms. Notwithstanding the worthiness of the social message, the process of recuperation of these value-challenges is exploitive and instrumental, a system of commodification, entirely indifferent to these values, is strengthened through its absorption and adaptation to challenge. Perhaps this accommodating commodification of values is the purest, cleanest and most insidious evolutionary source of human coercion.

Silence

An obsessive asphyxiating truth or a plurality of contingent self-serving truths are questionable alternatives.

But can architecture really say anything anyway, let alone concern itself with the truth? Is architecture ultimately only about itself and therefore open to multiple interpretations and representations as it is uses? Is architecture silent to questions of truth?

The adaptation and reuse of architecture for seemingly contradictory representations throughout history would seem to support this, from the Roman pagan basilicas adapted for Christian Churches through to endless classical colonnades and porticos for fascist representations of power and oppression, or monuments to democracy and freedom. Architecture seems in many ways ultimately value-free and available for adaptation to any use or ideological application.

Is architecture only ultimately about itself, is it entirely autonomous and is there perhaps within its silence some kind of truth? Is it through autonomy and independence that architecture might speak?

Through a self-referential architecture that draws on its own history, there is a possible separation that allows architectural form to be distanced from function, political and technological drivers. An architecture founded on a universal human project, composed from its typological and classical history. This autonomy and distancing are not necessarily neutral but potentially critical. Perhaps this was the remarkable ambition in the distilled work of Aldo Rossi; text, drawings, and an architecture of the city, of singular purpose. A true silence that allows architecture to stand apart and speak.

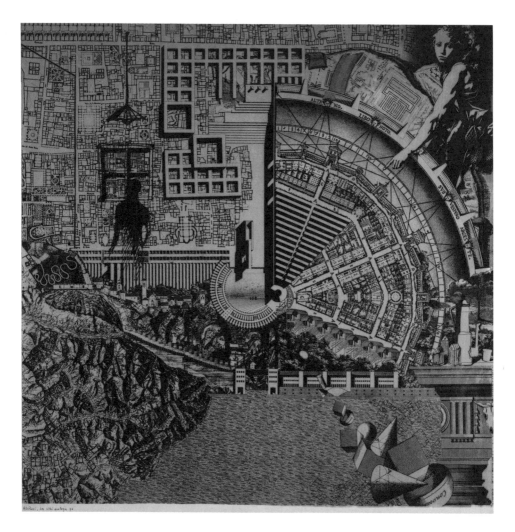

8 Aldo Rossi, Eraldo Consolascio, Bruno Reichlin, Fabio Reinhart, *Città Analoga*, 1976.

Classical architecture, through thousands of years of adaptation and intergenerational re-use, has been largely washed clean of ideological associations and can be seen as universal and fundamental in its elements and composition. A human universality that allows it to be autonomous and self-referential.

But such independence and transparency to ideology is euro-centric and difficult to entirely accept. Surely such adaptable classical modernist form is nothing but a representation of extreme oppression to First Nations cultures that have suffered the violence of invasion and colonial settlement.

Lies

Architecture cannot be entirely autonomous, it cannot be immune or completely indifferent to the functions and uses it accommodates, nor the political and ideological intentions behind its design.

We confer meaning on architecture through our intentions, our presence, our use and our ceremonies. Architecture is not entirely neutral to the human lives within it. It is marked by them and comes to embody the memory of these human lives and events. Both the celebrations and achievements, but also the pain and scars of our deeds, become embedded in the space and fabric of the architecture.

We have all felt this embodiment of life and deeds in spaces marked by great happiness and perhaps more powerfully in buildings that have witnessed and supported human suffering and pain. Architecture cannot be innocent of the deeds it has accommodated or the intentions for which it was constructed. It surely shares the guilt, and we can feel it in the walls, the windows, and the doors that have closed on such suffering.

Architecture will hold the memory of the intention behind its design and the witnessing of events for generations, both good and bad. Perhaps this is why some buildings must be retained and preserved while others must be demolished and erased.

Beyond such marks of memory, can architecture actually 'say' anything, true or false?

Despite many suggestions otherwise, architecture is not really a language and does not speak truth and falsehoods like language. But nor is it entirely mute.

Architecture can perhaps speak non-propositional truths. Truths that are beyond words and speak more directly to us and within us. Architecture does this through experience relating to almost all our senses, associations and memories. Architecture can figure and frame our experience of the world, reset and reorientate us.

3 Pablo Picasso in a statement made in Spanish to Marius de Zayas. Picasso approved de Zayas' manuscript before it was translated into English and published in the The Arts (New York, May 1923) under the title *Picasso Speaks*.

Architecture can make us see and feel the truth of the world through waking us from our slumber; through inspiring us, confronting us, reassuring us, wrapping arms around us, or turning us out to face the world.

Architecture does not tell these truths through some scenographic mask indifferent to the materials and nature of its making, nor by merely transparently reflecting the reality of its structure and construction. Architecture can explain the nature of its making, its assembly, a tectonic composition, then bend this representation for poetic intent. Weight can be made weightless, enclosure made open, solidity made transparent.

Architecture tells its truth through lies, distortions of construction for formal purpose. Lies that may help us glimpse truth about the world and our place in it. Architecture gives us an experience that distills our consciousness, concentrates our senses and perceptions to our interrelationship with each other and our world.

We can be slightly changed through this experience, perhaps see the world slightly differently, perhaps feel a truth of our interrelationship with the world around us, and maybe even begin to reconcile our place in it.

We all know that Art is not truth. Art is a lie that makes us realise the truth, at least the truth that is given to us to understand. The artist must know the manner whereby to convince others of the truthfulness of his lies.

Pablo Picasso [3]

9 Pablo Picasso, *Grande Baigneuse au livre*, 1937.

The Slowness of Architecture and the Speed of the Architect

These rules, the sign language and grammar of the Game, constitute a kind of highly developed secret language drawing upon several sciences and arts, but especially mathematics and music (and/or musicology), and capable of expressing and establishing interrelationships between the content and conclusions of nearly all scholarly disciplines. The Glass Bead Game is thus a mode of playing with the total contents and values of our culture; it plays with them as, say, in the great age of the arts a painter might have played with the colours on his palette.

Hermann Hesse, *The Glass Bead Game* (1943) [1]

1 Hermann Hesse; translated from the German *Das Glasperlenspiel* by Richard and Clara Winston, *The Glass Bead Game*, 1943.

10 John Travolta and Samuel L. Jackson as Vincent Vega and Jules Winnfield in Quentin Tarantino's *Pulp Fiction*, 1994.

Quentin Tarantino, the writer and director of two landmark films, *Reservoir Dogs* and *Pulp Fiction*, has been acclaimed as one of the most influential film-makers of our time. Tarantino has detected that speech at speed becomes abstract, a kind of self-referential language game. He presents our conversation as a language game centred around consumerist trivia and product obsession, and illustrates our exceptional ability to say nothing at pedantic length. Interlaced within these flat, continuous, and humorous language games, and seemingly almost more trivial than the content of the conversation, are acts of extreme violence, which disturbingly somehow also seem funny. This distinctive mix of immediacy, consumerist obsession, and extreme violence skillfully interwoven by Tarantino has become a defining expression of contemporary western culture, where our artwork is emptied of all content, stripped of all politics, metaphysics, moral and ethical interest. Tarantino's films in some ways mirror the conditions and 'values' of our contemporary life disconnected from the concreteness of existence, where we are more interested in the price of consumables than questions of being.

The cultural context of our contemporary post-modern crises is an emphasis on the signifier over the signified, and language over being. We have rejected the utopian meta-theories of modernism with its logocentric domination of metaphysics as oppressive ideology, and we seem to have overcome modernity's existential crisis through simple acquiescence and distraction from our alienation. Alienation no longer bothers us; we accept and indulge in our isolation and separateness. We are suspended within disconnected, universalising zones of consumption and mobility to float above a ground beyond our interest, freed from heaviness, content, and meaning, absorbing ourselves with appearances, immediacy, and image. Only the most extreme acts of transgression, of human violence and environmental vandalism will momentarily disturb us from our abstract floatation.

Our weightless, consumerist, self-absorption is supported through a proliferation of information and communication technology, that breeds an insistence on immediacy and speed.

Information and data are now accumulating faster than any material or artefact the world has ever seen before and they are expanding at an exponential rate. But notwithstanding these vast quantities and the speed of information, it can never be enough; we want more and faster.

We are overwhelmed by information, more than we can possibly deal with, to the extent that it rolls over us with no time to distinguish between fact, opinion and deception. It brings with it the expectation and illusion of efficiency and speed of response that now invades every aspect and space of our lives. Our home and work are now indistinguishable portals for the immediacy of data and response, while the digital self-image has become our dominant identity. Speed and immediacy have become not means, but ends in themselves, such that the object of this vast media and information production and exchange is lost, and time similarly is drained away through endless processing, seemingly without purpose. We are all living longer and yet through this speed, intensity and immediacy, our lives seem consumed and reduced.

Our worldwide network of communications with all its associated image, voice and text portal devices, has created a system that connects us all within a single system of exchange, at the same time as it separates and isolates us. We are all now provided the opportunity to have our say, but is this freedom of speech, a liberating expansion of democracy and inclusion or merely the ultimate polarising babel-fest where everyone can have their say, have their opinion reinforced, choose their facts, feel self-righteous and ultimately be ignored?

We have become locked into a system of endless information production and exchange. In every aspect of our lives the immediacy of information exchange seems both desired by us and subjected upon us. We have become data junkies unable to distinguish the labouring of work-life from the labouring of home-life. Having our say, processing and exchanging information as quickly as possible has become our objective and our obsession. Hardly anyone actually makes anything anymore.

This is also true of the architect, buried under the proliferation of images and information. But the work of the architect, while abstracted to a large extent, is finally and emphatically directed towards the actual making and construction of buildings; this is surely our purpose.

Building processes themselves have actually changed relatively little, they are not significantly quicker, but the speed and volume of information surrounding the production have increased exponentially. Projects are now developed within a sea of information, more and more information is required to build a building and despite the apparent speed with which it travels, the sheer volume seems to more than consume any time saved. Project management, web-based information management and process management systems, building integrated modelling, quality assurance systems, approval and submission processes and systems, more and more information and processes now surrounds our projects. But is the work much better and is it quicker, or more compromised, more wasteful?

Speed frequently wastes that which we hold most precious and that which it was supposed to overcome—time. We rush more hectically, transmit information ever more quickly and in greater volume, but paradoxically, have less and less time. Speed, change, and efficiency now seem to be values in themselves, ends rather than means. Our world is dominated by the angel of speed. It is a world of consumerist obsession, where our needs are so completely transformed and distorted by media and advertising that we crave what is current and immediate, follow the dictates of fashion, and measure the success of Christmas through consumer spending.

Quentin Tarantino expresses all this perfectly, demonstrating that what is of interest to us is not any 'loss of being' but the speed and efficiency with which we can clean out the car after the violence, or perhaps more importantly, the quality of the coffee.

So, what is the place of architecture, if not wholly integrated into this market system of consumerist products?

The architectural landscape of our contemporary condition has emerged from a period of post-modern heterogeneity towards a greater homogeneity that may be related to the processes of globalisation and represent an apparent return to a form of modernism.

Is this really a return to the modern project of human emancipation and liberation? Or is this 'return to modernity' better understood as merely the predictable swing of the market pendulum of fashion. A retro-modernism now exploiting our ironic nostalgia for a century past, Brutalist concrete finally cool again. A mere updating of syntax relative to market opportunity acknowledging and accepting the reduction of architecture to designer-product, more form than content. Is this return to modernity simply reflective of general exhaustion with the endless images of a post-modernism that seem now fleeting, more difficult, and weaker than we first imagined?

In any event what of the irony of notions of 'return' to modernity, how can it be possible when returning is a contradiction to the essence of modernity which by its nature is directed only towards the future. The avant-garde is by definition directed forward and must not risk turning from the future to look back on the wreckage. Is not a return to modernity a contradiction in terms?

Our contemporary international modernism seems linked more to the processes and ideology of globalisation and associated technological developments than the aspirations of the Modern Project. Much of this work is characterised by fully glazed forms, facetted and shaped this way and that, seeking our attention but also projecting an insubstantial transiency, and an almost conscious lack of substance. It may well be that the forces of the market, globalisation and consumerism, are now being presented without any rhetoric of place, history, or radical protest, and without any false pretense of meaning. This may be the first step towards a more authentic and critical contemporary architecture, or it may merely represent a simple acceptance and acquiescence.

11 Airports, shopping malls, hotels, and other transit zones are non-places, of consumption and mobility, encouraging thoughtless, constant action, and offering no moment nor place to stay.

The context of this work is a contemporary world that is characterised by non-place, pseudo-public realms, and consumption disguised as community or individual expression. It may well be that the expanding horizon of our knowledge and extension of our possibilities through the electronic media make the world, in a sense, more accessible, more familiar, but at the same time, this extended territory is less and less meaningful. All the more often we experience a zone or space where we interface or intersect in some fleeting social simulation at speed, rather than the experience of a place in which to be and meet.

Airports, shopping malls, hotels, and other transit zones are non-places of consumption and mobility, encouraging thoughtless, constant action, and offering no moment nor place to stay. Even our image-conscious apartment/retail complexes are more investment locations, designer products, and frames in which to be seen, rather than places to be.

We have an overwhelming amount of information, stimulation, simulation, individualisation and speed, but so little sense of being, community, or place, and so little time.

2 Hal Foster, *Recodings: Art, Spectacle, Cultural Politics, Part II:(Post)Modern Polemics, Readings in Cultural Resistance*, p.157 Seattle, Washington: Bay Press, 1985.

3 Franco Moretti, *Signs Taken for Wonders*, London: Verso, 2005.

Architecture of all the arts has the most direct and unmediated relationship with the economy and society itself. While western society has experienced many changes and transformations since the industrial revolution, the basic organising and over-riding principle of social and economic life have remained the capitalist production of profit. The attraction of Capitalism, is not difficult to understand, the private accumulation of wealth and individualism are powerful influences and capitalist modernisation has achieved real and positive gains for society: Life spans have increased, economic growth has expanded at incredible rates, contact between different societies through the formation of the world market, and new cultural possibilities brought about by the creation of new wants and need, and perhaps most importantly, the possibility of broader access to wealth and technology.

However, all this has been achieved at considerable cost to humanity, in the form of violence, oppression, inequity and the destruction of tradition, as the valuation of all activity has been reduced to the calculation of profit.

The massive upheaval, social violence, and conflict of capitalism have historically been mediated through the operation of ideology. Ideology understood as a distortion of reality, or justifying mask to specific interest, or perhaps best as Hal Foster suggests, 'the limitation of thought in such a way that social conflicts and historical contradictions are, magically resolved.'[2] It has proved to be a flexible and responsive ideology sliding underneath contemporary Neo-Liberalism, with its embrace of free-trade privatisation and deregulation, as well as Social Liberalism's prioritising of individual freedom in partnership with social and economic development.

However, a quite separate reconciliation of the human conflicts within capitalism is attempted by culture. Throughout the late nineteenth century and early twentieth-century, our art attempted to reconcile the irreconcilable and frequently either confronted or tried to compensate for our modern alienated condition.

As Franca Moretti remarks:

12 Mark Rothko, *No. 2 (Blue Red Green)*, 1953.

While capitalist society is unthinkable without the scientific and technical progress reflected in the separation of intellect and morality, it is equally unthinkable without the incessant attempt to annul that separation and remedy it, an attempt to which the extraordinary and apparently inexplicable proliferation of aesthetic activities that distinguishes capitalism bears witness.[3]

4 Fredric Jameson, 'Architecture and the Critique of Ideology' in Architecture Criticism Ideology, ed. Joan Ockman pp. 77, Princeton: Princeton University Press, 1985.

5 Manfredo Tafuri and Francesco Dal Co, Modern Architecture, Milan: Electa Editrice, 1976.

During the Modernist period, the critical reconciliation offered by art and architecture maintained its separation from the instrumental operation of ideology, only through turning inwards and exploring increased abstraction, in an attempt to get behind the surface and the immediate, to reveal essential meaning.

However, as art and architecture became increasingly withdrawn, capitalism, through the development of mass media, advertising and technology, began to penetrate previously uncommodified areas. To the extent that in advanced capitalism, culture is no longer a separate reconciliatory and possibly critical force but is fully integrated with the operation of capital. Culture is commodified and extended through mass media to penetrate our unconscious. Such a complete infestation of commodification may even allow the disappearance of ideology as Fredric Jameson has observed:

The practices of consumption and consumerism themselves become enough to reproduce and legitimise the system, no matter what 'ideology' you happen to be committed to. No abstract ideas, beliefs, ideologies, or philosophical systems, but rather immanent practices of daily life may now occupy the functional position of 'ideology' within a purified Advanced Capitalism.[4]

The point at which modern abstraction and the ability of architecture and culture to be a reconciliatory force independent of capitalist ideology reached its limit, can perhaps be located with the construction of the Seagram Building on Park Avenue, New York in 1958. As revealed by Manfredo Tafuri:

The 'almost nothing' became a 'big glass' ...reflecting images of the urban chaos that surrounds the timeless Miesian purity ...It accepts (the shift and flux of phenomena), absorbs them to themselves in a perverse multi-duplication, like a Pop Art sculpture arrives at the ultimate limits of its own possibilities. Like the last notes sounded by the Doctor Faustus of Thomas Mann, alienation, having become absolute, testifies uniquely to its own presence, separating itself from the world to declare the world's incurable malady.[5]

13 Mies van der Rohe and Philip Johnson, Segram Building, New York, 1958.

6 Milan Kundera; translated from the French by Linda Asher, *Slowness*, London: Faber & Faber, 1996.

What does this mean for our contemporary return to modernity? How do the minimalist images of neo-modernism relate to the confrontation of Mies van der Rohe's sublime and poetic declaration of our poverty?

One of the great paradigms of modernity that changed dimension around this decisive moment is speed.

For modernity at the beginning of the twentieth-century speed was like the machine, a symbol, an expression of progress and confidence in the future. The slipstream, aerodynamic forms, buildings firmly in the ground yet given the visual potential to accelerate. An aesthetic of speed projected an image or poetic vision of a reality not yet present, a poetic anticipation of the effect of modernisation and technology.

But speed lost its poetic relevance as high-speed trains, cars, rockets, and aeroplanes brought with them pollution, environmental damage, climate crises, urban degradation, and gridlock. The speed of objects and people, that was the obsession and symbol of modernity; gave way, as did modernism itself, to the speed of information.

But what is the speed of architecture?

Is it not generally stationary and seeking some kind of permanence. Or is architecture, reduced to the surface skin of a neutral construction to be updated with fashion, traveling at a market-driven speed, where occasionally, if neglected long enough will become fashionable again. Or can this reduction of architecture to mere consumables be resisted?

And what, if there was a poetic aesthetic of speed with early modernism, could possibly be a poetic aesthetic of slowness? More importantly, if speed rarely saves time, why is it our obsession, why do we thirst for speed and treat slowness with contempt?

Milan Kundera in his novel *Slowness* gives a possible explanation.

14 The man hunched over his motor-cycle can focus only on the present instant of his flight.

...the man hunched over his motorcycle can focus only on the present instant of his flight; he is caught in a fragment of time cut off from both the past and the future; he is wrenched from the continuity of time; he is outside time; in other words, he is in a state of ecstasy. In that state he is unaware of his age, his wife, his children, his worries, and so he has no fear, because the source of fear is in the future, and a person freed of the future has nothing to fear.

Speed is the form of ecstasy the technical revolution has bestowed on man. As opposed to a motorcyclist, the runner is always present in his body, forever required to think about his blisters, his exhaustion; when he runs, he feels his weight, his age, more conscious than ever of himself and of his time of life. This all changes when man delegates the faculty of speed to a machine: from then on, his own body is outside the process, and he gives over to a speed that is non-corporeal, non-material, pure speed, speed itself, ecstasy speed.[6]

7 Ibid.

And later:

There is a secret bond between slowness and memory, between speed and forgetting. Consider this utterly commonplace situation: a man is walking down the street. At a certain moment, he tries to recall something, but the recollection escapes him. Automatically, he slows down. Meanwhile, a person who wants to forget a disagreeable incident he has just lived through starts unconsciously to speed up his pace, as if he were trying to distance himself from a thing still too close to him in time.

In existential mathematics, that experience takes the form of two basic equations: the degree of slowness is directly proportional to the intensity of memory; the degree of speed is directly proportional to the intensity of forgetting.[7]

A profound fear and need to forget, explain our obsession with speed. We rush to forget our loss of being, to forget our lost sense of dwelling, to forget our homelessness, our alienation. We speed because we have nowhere to stop.

Non-dwelling is now the essential characteristic of contemporary life. The home and dwelling are past, are no longer possible. Perhaps therefore, it is the silent architecture of Mies van der Rohe that can escape ideology and mystification through a seeming indifference to dwelling, a deeply poetic testament to its absence. Developing from this, only a contemporary architecture that reflects the impossibility of dwelling can succeed in obtaining a form of authenticity.

The Farnsworth House in Illinois, constructed shortly before the Seagram Building in 1951, is a clear acknowledgement of our non-dwelling. Within the Farnsworth House 'liberated' humanity is suspended from the world in which it can no longer dwell. The sparse and purified platforms permit no masks of comforting self-deception, but instead confront us with the reality of our estrangement. While the natural world is preserved only through emphatic separation from our corrupting presence.

This may be a negative artwork or a negative place to begin, but it is importantly, an authentic, revelation of our impoverishment: We cannot dwell, we can only 'stay' somewhere, for a moment, and begin to confront our homelessness.

If there is the opportunity for an authentic reexamination of the modern project within contemporary conditions, then the basic objective of modernity, that of human emancipation and liberation, must be reevaluated and the question asked as to how such a project is now recoverable and even possible.

The place of architecture within such a revised project must not only begin from an acknowledgement of our homelessness, our alienation, but also develop from an understanding of architecture's susceptibility to commodity reduction and ideological influence. Mere update in syntax has to be rejected through an understanding of the depth of architecture's representative nature beyond surface effects and image.

Through architecture as the creation of critical constructs through which to understand and interpret the world, we must somehow resolve our place in it. We can begin from the negative, from confirmation of our homelessness and our alienation. But architecture is fundamentally an attempt to reconcile our human presence in the world, surely this is its ultimate project.

15 Glenn Murcutt, Marika-Alderton
House, Eastern Arnhem Land,
Northern Territory, 1990-94.

The houses of Glenn Murcutt hovering over their bushland sites develop a similar acknowledgement of our estrangement to Mies's Farnsworth House. We are suspended and separated from a world we can only corrupt. But there is another dimension to the form, space and fabric of these buildings; there is a kind of poetic longing, to be part of, to belong. An empathy is sought with the land and with the trees, but the separation is empathetic.

In Murcutt's work, there is at once a representation and acknowledgements of our homelessness, but also an expression of our deep desire to once again know what it is to dwell. We are suspended because while we wish so much to be brought to ground, we fear destroying it with our touch.

16 Jørn Utzon, Can Lis House,
Mallorca, Spain, 1972.

Jørn Utzon's first house in Porto Petro, Mallorca, seems to go one step further. Remarkably Utzon seems to have been able to create one place for us to stay. Here it seems it may actually be possible for us to momentarily belong, momentarily stop. It does not violate or stand apart from its site, it is the site. It has a primordial quality but lies within the project of modernity. It is at once ancient and modern.

Interestingly, both Murcutt and Utzon are architects who have practiced outside the norm and occupy the margin. Neither could be described as efficient. They are outside the market, resist commercial reality, and have been stung by it. They are also slow.

The ideology of our time with its emphasis on efficiency, change, the free market, and speed, is in many ways the antithesis of the necessary conditions for making architecture.

Architecture is not efficient, in fact, it is often how efficiency has been subordinated to other values that distinguishes architecture.

Architecture is not mere change, architecture is more a perpetual transformation towards permanence, it is more often about uncovering what it is in humanity that does not change.

Architecture does not move at speed, as any of us know who has tried to make architecture.

Architecture is slow.

The Face of Architecture and the Mask of the Architect

A great building must begin with the immeasurable, must go through measurable means when it is being designed, and in the end must be unmeasured.

Louis Kahn [1]

1 Louis Kahn, quoted in *The Note-books and Drawings of Louis I. Kahn.* ed. Richard S. Wurman and Eugene Feldman. Philadelphia: Falcon Press, 1962.

17 The face gives us the perfect innocence and open future of a child, as well as the lines and marks of age and wisdom, both essential to understanding and finally accepting the mortal nature of life rather than merely measuring its duration.

Surely the façade is the very essence of the architect's art, and the projection of architecture into the public street, public square or natural landscape. More than any other element of the architect's craft, this must be ours, to draw and compose a vision and aspiration of our community and of our time.

Or maybe not.

Façade engineering and building envelope performance is now dominant in architecture. We are surrounded by specialists, technicians and experts in the design, production and construction of architectural envelopes. These engineering specialists measure, compute and analyse, a vast array of data about the enclosing surfaces of our buildings. They calculate the performance of our design in terms of: Visible Light Transmittance (VLT), thermal transmittance U-value, solar radiation, Solar Heat Gain Coefficient (SHGC), reflectivity, glare, watertightness and systems of performance coatings and membranes, material science and technology, energy transfer, exchange and generation, and so on. A proliferation of important data and enough to alienate architects to such an extent that we could be forgiven for just stepping back and selecting a Double Glazed Unit (DGU) glazing colour (very limited), and the framing colour (seemingly limitless).

This complex data matrix, when combined with the increasing regulation of the building envelope, in similar terms, but using blunt instruments such NCC Section J and BASIX,[2] in many ways reduces the surfaces of architecture to a mere set of performance numbers. Of course, the technical performance of the architectural envelope is important, essential in fact, but there is a risk in our increasing focus of this data-driven design, committees and expert design review that we undermine the essential nature of our art and the very heart of architecture, that we forsake the immeasurable with an obsession for only the measurable. The easy allure of quantification makes comparison and assessment simple, but perhaps misses the point.

I recently spoke at a Façade Engineering conference that embodied the technical depth and specialisation of this expanding field of expertise.

2 Australian Building Codes Board, *The National Construction Code NCC, Section J*, <https://ncc.abcb.gov.au>, 2021. Department of Planning, Industry and Environment, NSW Government, *BASIX,<https://www.planningportal.nsw.gov.au/basix>*, 2021.

At this event, it was all agreed that the future of façade engineering is in the balance of 'technology' and 'sustainable design'. But what I noticed was that notwithstanding the very technical, measurable and technological nature of the conference, it was called 'Façade' engineering and I wondered why? It seems far more appropriate to call it say, 'Built Envelope' engineering, but we persist with using the seemingly antiquated term façade and even use the ç cedilla latin script.

The word comes from the French foreign loan word façade, which in turn comes from the Italian facciata, from faccia meaning 'face', ultimately from post-classical Latin facia. The earliest usage recorded by the Oxford English Dictionary is 1656.

The façade is the 'face' of architecture.

The human face is the model of our façades. Now of course the elements and composition of the human face is filled with functional and performance rationale. The opening of the eyes for light and sight, filtered and focused through an exquisitely rational arrangement of cornea, pupil, iris and lens. The eyes paired for three-dimensional perspective and sheltered from sun, sweat and rain with the brows and the muscular contraction of the squint. The nose opening profiled and orientated to shelter and allow easy intake of oxygen and expel of carbon dioxide and detect scent. And of course, a most flexible, sensitive and adaptive opening for communication and the consumption of energy. The face is a high-performance technical wonder. But this is not what we see or even look for in a human face. Eyes are not merely for looking out of, they are for looking into, deeply, windows into our character and even our soul. The balance, composition, perfection and most importantly the imperfection, the quirk of character affect us most deeply, tells us more than the words we hear, silently connects with us, inspires us and joins us.

The face gives us the perfect innocence and open future of a child, as well as the lines and marks of age and wisdom, both essential to understanding and finally accepting the mortal nature of life rather than merely measuring its duration.

18 Louis Kahn, Arts United Center, Fort Wayne, Indiana, 1973.

In these faces, we will see beauty, pain, grief, courage, hopes and aspirations.

Similarly, the face or façade of our architecture is far more than the measurements of its environmental mediation and efficiency. The façade is a composed representation of our collective aspirations and values. Whether the architect intends it or not, conscious or unconscious, the façade expresses and represents. It is the face of the building, it will reflect the aspiration and ambitions that have given life and form to architecture.

Making, constructing, composing is such an integral act of our human experience, it is, in a sense, an extension of our life and a seeking to join more deeply with the world we inhabit. Anthropomorphism is the most direct reflection of this essential human psychology, we make our works like us, reflections of us, imbue them with a sense of life. Perhaps this is a way in which we want to extend our own lives or come to know the life around us better. It is a paradoxical act of both asserting ourselves on the world and an act of discovery, searching for meaning and life in the matter of the world.

Such anthropomorphism can be thin and literal, comical even if composed with a straight face, the façade becoming a cartoon-like representation,

81

3 Leon Battista Alberti; translated by Joseph Rykwert, Robert Tavernor and Neil Leach, *De re aedificatoria (On the Art of Building)*, Cambridge, Massachusetts: MIT Press, 1988.

sometimes unintended, sometimes unexpected in the hand of the maker. But even such literal compositions of the human face making an appearance within an abstract field can surprise and move us deeply, can be subliminal until pointed out and perhaps is so innate as to have escaped the consciousness of the maker. There is surely something essentially human, perhaps even culturally universal to this anthropomorphism and reach for interconnection with the world.

Architecture and its faces has the capacity to represent the nature and depth of our collective values and ideas. It does not do this like language but through direct experience in the way it frames our relationship with the world. The making of architecture is an act of not only shelter and inhabitation of the world, but of our search to find our place in this world, a search for a meaningful symbiosis.

At some point the way we think about façades, the way in which they can represent us and the way they are constructed fundamentally changed.

This moment perhaps first occurred in Florence in 1451 with the construction of Palazzo Rucellai designed by Leon Battista Alberti. This was the birth of modernity, when a fracture began to develop that separated the surface of architecture from its construction, intellect from craft, image, or appearance from the reality of making and theory from practice. Alberti did not rise through the guilds or trades; his interest in architecture was primarily intellectual. His famous treatise on architecture contain no illustrations; architecture was to be thought, idealised and theorised.[3]

Alberti placed great emphasis on the idealised representational role of the façade most clearly expressed in the Palazzo Rucellai, where an idealised conception is applied over the actual reality of its assembly and construction.

The stone construction of the façade economically conforms to the restriction of the block size and coursing but is completely masked through the application of an independent veneer that geometrically idealises and represents.

19 Right: Le Corbusier, Chapelle Notre Dame Du Haut, Ronchamp, 1954.

83

20 Leon Alberti Battista, Palazzo
Rucellai, Florence, Italy, 1451.

The face became a mask and, in a sense, gave birth to the second definition of the word 'façade' as something thin and superficial that disguises or conceals: An appearance of integrity and depth that was ultimately a mere 'façade'.

Architecture has continued to struggle with the duality of surface/depth, face/mask since this moment and responded in a number of ways.

From a modernist abstraction that turns inwards, separating from the world of myth and tradition in an autonomous search for more universal values, silencing the façade through absolute formalism in order to remain 'true', to a Venturi-like embrace of this separation that frees architecture from the weight of its making so that it can become, a sign, a sculpture, or a mere image of what used to be architecture.

When this duality of the façade, dislocated from its making and form, is combined with the intense media proliferation and market driven consumption of images, the perfect storm of architectural commodification is born, and its blinding pull is very difficult to escape. Resistance to this reductive pull is one of the greatest challenges of the contemporary architect, but it is essential to the restoration of the holistic nature of our craft. Perhaps a good place to start is to seek a rejoining of the façade with its form and construction in the cause of representing and interpreting our contemporary values, ideas and aspirations within a progressive tradition of making architecture.

This means an embrace of technology and technique, new materials and innovation, and above all a closeness, and empathy with our industry of fabrication and construction, as this is the very medium of our art. But a qualified one. Not only in the service of efficiency, sustainability index and envelope performance; the measurable, but also in the service of cultural/social purpose, narrative, meaning and interpretation; the immeasurable.

It means also to give life to our work, and through it to help frame, reconcile and even atone our presence in this world.

The Nature of Architecture and the Extinction of the Architect

What have they done to the earth?
What have they done to our fair sister?
Ravaged and plundered and ripped her and bit her
Stuck her with knives in the side of the dawn
And tied her with fences and dragged her down.

Jim Morrison, *When The Music's Over* (1967) [1]

[1] Jim Morrison, lead singer of The Doors, 'When The Music's Over,' *Strange Days*, Elektra Records, 1967.

21 Ruins of the Temple of Jupiter in
Pompeii with Mount Vesuvius in the
background.

Sustainability

The sustainability of our natural environment is perhaps the most critical issue of our time. Almost every day we read of new dimensions to this crisis; melting ice caps, unprecedented bush fires, rising sea levels and global warming, all increasing at faster rates than first predicted. The contemporary human way of life, our settlement patterns, animal life and the character of the natural world, are all under threat.

But what do we mean when we talk of sustainability in this way, and more importantly what are we seeking to sustain and preserve?

Is it the whole of the natural world, the landscape the oceans and the multitude of life? But this is always in a state of flux, always changing and adapting even to our extreme destructive actions, nature will respond, reclaim, and transform.

Is it more about us, is it humanity that must be persevered? Yet again it is unlikely we will all be lost, although our settlement and civilisation maybe dramatically and disturbingly transformed.

The Club of Rome produced a more exact objective in the report of 1972 'Limits to Growth'. It sought a world system that is:

1. sustainable without sudden and uncontrolled collapse; and
2. capable of satisfying the basic material requirements of all of its people.[2]

In 1987 this was refined by the Brundtland Report 'Our Common Future' to be sustainable development, defined as "development that meets the needs of the present without compromising the ability of future generations to meet their own needs."[3]

What is the nature of these 'basic material requirements' or intergenerational 'needs'? In the West, notwithstanding the extreme social inequality, we have moved way beyond basic, to a form of excessive consumption well beyond need.

2 Donella H. Meadows, Dennis L. Meadows, Jørgen Randers, William W. Behrens III, *The Limits to Growth: A report for the Club of Rome's project on the predicament of mankind*, p.158 New York: Universe Books, 1972.

3 World Commission on Environment and Development United Nations, *Our Common Future also known as the Brundtland Report*, p.26, New York and Oxford: Oxford University Press, 1987.

22 Ceiba tree ruin in Angkor Wat Temple complex in Cambodia.

Is it then sustaining our present way of life and levels of consumption, economic and population growth? Is this realistic or even desirable?

And what is sustainable architecture in this context, how does it fit into our human needs? Is it a maintenance of our current market-defined levels of image production, consumption and urban renewal on an exponential scale?

Or is it a form of architecture that mitigates environmental damage, or even heals and reforms our essential interrelationship with the world, its landscape and places?

Architcture and Nature

Architecture was central to making our place in this world, this is its purpose and nature from the moment we struggled into existence, pushing and pulling at the earth, trees and rocks to make a place for us; to make a safe settlement with access to water and resources; and to make a settlement that supported and figured the social and political life of our society in relation to this place. Architecture is in many ways a natural extension of the landscape, a human adjustment and reconfiguration of the topography. Architecture is made by us, but also made by nature. Architecture and nature are inseparable.

This integral and synonymous interrelation of architecture and nature was a sustainable form of settlement for our environment, for our world, but ultimately not necessarily for us. If the resources dried up, if nature turned against us—with storms, or earthquake, or drought—then we were no longer sustained, we were lost, and our architecture was laid ruin and reclaimed by the earth from which it seemed to rise. It was nature that was sustained, always.

The more we built with awareness of nature, the climate, the ground and the spirit of a place, the more sustainable our settlement and the more at peace we were in a sense of interconnection and belonging. But always we were dependent on nature's will, and we remained potential victims of its vagaries and the threat of perdition.

23 Skyscrapers on Bunker Hill, in Downtown Los Angeles, USA.

Modernity and Crisis

Modernity seemed to offer us a final release from this threat. Spiritual release, as we could now stand alone, freed from restraining mythology of the land; and physical release, as the vast technical and scientific developments that followed this independence gave us great power over our environment. We were now free, the tables were turned, and we could subjugate nature to our will, our vagaries. Our instruments and machines finally enabling the taming of a recalcitrant landscape with all its climatic idiosyncrasies and rebellions.

Architecture was empowered in new directions through modernity's dizzying technological developments: we could build tall and wide, travel via elevator and escalators, mechanical ventilation, heating and air conditioning freeing us from the climatic locale and artificial lighting opening up deep interior spaces for occupation. Windows were replaced with sealed curtain walls, depth and weight with thinness and flatness. Finally, the functional simplicity of the glazed box evolved triumphant and became hegemonic in the late twentieth-century.

Architecture disconnected from its true nature came to resemble a form of building engineering. The measurable and quantifiable were prioritised within a reductive ideology of functionalist architecture. Architecture lost its essential nature and architects became more comfortable talking of services and structural engineering, space and functional quantification, rather than the human interrelationship with the world. It was a triumph of technology and technique, ignited by our ontologically release from the natural world, that in turn remade and flattened this landscape into a universal pattern of instrumental settlement on a breathtaking global scale.

Place, as an embodiment of meaningful human interconnection with the natural landscape, was replaced by extended, synthetic spaces for movement, efficiency and exchange; a placelessness that fuelled a needless hyper-consumption to distract us from our loss. This destructive suppression and eradication of place and locale was complemented by an insidious and potentially catastrophic undermining of the life balance of the natural world.

Climate change, global warming, mass extinction and environmental destruction. The symptoms of this environmental catastrophe became only all too measurable and we all finally began to feel them.

Slowly a state of crisis and urgency has developed prompting a focus on the reduction of carbon emissions and combatting temperature rises now presenting the key imperative. This is the preeminent contemporary challenge to architecture, a crisis long in the making and too long neglected.

Architecture and Crisis

The industry turned, in 1998 The World Green Building Council was founded, specialist engineering disciplines of environmental engineering formed, together with a series of performance indexes by which we now measure the sustainability performance of the project, assess, rate and score. LEED, BREEAM, Greenstar, NABERS and a new green lexicon of how we describe our work developed. Supported by government regulation, market and community expectations, these rating indexes play an important role in architecture's response to this crisis. The evolving nature of indexes and regulation extending into areas such as embodied energy and embodied carbon are slowly reducing the construction and operational energy and carbon emissions with zero and carbon positive outcomes.

However, while this quantification, engineering and measurable dimension of environmental sustainability is part of architecture, it is not architecture and not all that architecture needs to do in response to this environment challenge.

We should make sure we do not merely extend the reductive modernist engineering lexicon of architecture and simply adjust the measurable performance of our constructions. Nor should we merely fall into the marketable production of 'green' imaging, such as superficial green hanging gardens or displays of sustainable elements and equipment, to decorate these assemblies.

We need to recognise and remember the path that brought us to this crisis.

The essential nature of architecture is one with the environment. The sustainability of the natural environment is inherent in the nature of architecture; they are the same.

Architecture is the interconnection of humanity with the natural world. It is the window, the bridge, the boundary, the threshold, the framing between us and the world. It mediates and sustains an interrelationship.

24 Fire engulfs bushland south of Black Head back beach, 2019.

The tragic ubiquitous mechanically-serviced glass office boxes of the twentieth-century are not architecture. Any building that damages and undermines our symbiosis with the natural world is not architecture. Building, development and construction perhaps, but not architecture.

Architecture is the framing of our lives in relation to the world we inhabit. It is an essential and artistic reach for a kind of symbiosis with our world; the bending of nature to accommodate us, and a bending of our nature to support the natural world.

Most importantly there is an essential poetic dimension to this interrelationship that cannot be reduced to scientific measures of environmental impacts—that is not enough. To find our peace, to reconcile our place, is not merely a matter of avoiding irreparable damage to our world, is not merely the pragmatic sustaining of our existence. It is finding and feeling a meaningful symbiosis that will endure.

The creation of architecture that interprets and figures our interrelationship with each other and our world is essential to this symbiosis and sense of peace.

4 Oodgeroo Noonuccal; Kath Walker, 'We Are Going' from the book of the same name *We are going : poems*, p.25, Brisbane: Jacaranda Press, 1964.

To make an architecture that finds a commonality across our varied cultures. Works that will endure, be retained and adapted for generations, because of their inherent humanity and meaning, is surely among the most cogent act of the architect. These works are not merely sustained because of convenience and durability, but because they reveal and support our balance in the world, give meaning and explanation to the search for our place within it, and offer a promise of peace.

We leave our markings in the earth, in a landscape transformed by us, but unless these are gentle markings true to the nature of the earth itself, then they will be washed away, and nature will reclaim and correct our work.

So somewhere in this process we must find an adjustment to the concept of 'ownership' of the land. It is not ours, nor indeed our future generation's, collectively or privately. Somehow, we will find a recognition that we are inseparable from and interdependent on the natural world, the landscape and life around us, that perhaps it owns us, or better, is us.

We are nature and the past, all the old ways
Gone now and scattered.
The scrubs are gone, the hunting and the laughter.
The eagle is gone, the emu and the kangaroo are gone
from this place.
The bora ring is gone.
The corroboree is gone.
And we are going.

Oodgeroo Noonuccal (1964) [4]

25 Aunty Oodgeroo Noonuccal,
Stradbroke Island, Queensland, ca.
1975.

The Fall
of the Architect

*To dare is to lose one's footing momentarily.
Not to dare is to lose oneself.*

Søren Kierkegaard [1]

1 Attributed to Søren Kierkegard.

26 Edge of the gargoyle, Chrysler
Building, New York.

In some ways is seems natural for us to seek high ground, to be drawn to the ridge, to the hilltop. This may be a simple expression of our collective sense of insecurity, because high ground is easier to defend and from its viewpoint, it is easier to see the approaching threats, be they from nature or each other. But then again, we are also more visible, venerable and exposed on this high ground.

Or is it simply the attraction of vista, an expansive perspective and connection with the horizon; our world, influence and experience extended through elevation.

Or perhaps it is the metaphoric human reach for the heavens and a sense of the sublime that draws us to build tall and climb the mountain. Up here we are closer to God. This escape from the ground understood as the natural path for a humanity cruelly thrown down to suffering on a threatening earth.

These deep human instincts are surely behind the architect's enduring obsession with height, with building as tall as possible. These embedded instincts perhaps combined with the technical challenge of defeating gravity, the paradoxical questioning of God's most basic law, in order to reach... well, God.

For the architect building tall seems to have been a powerful obsession and some ultimate measure of success, from the competitive medieval towers of San Gimignano, to the definition of a true modern city through the height and number of its architect's towers. These towers still seem to be the pinnacle for the aspiration and meaning of architects' professional work, from Ayn Rand's mythical ideal in Howard Roark, to our contemporary international masters.

But as our architects build tall and climb the scaffolding to stand atop of these synthetic mountains to admire both the extent of the breathtaking view and the consequential visibility of the majestic architectural creation itself, the edge of the scaffolding, the edge of the void touching these great towers, will beckon.

27 Edge of the scaffold, construction site, London.

If you stand on the roof or terrace of a tall building, you are naturally and irresistibly drawn to the parapet or balustrade. Something compels you to step right up to that edge, to lean over, against your better judgement, you feel a seemingly natural invitation to step over and out into that void, a feeling like an intuition that pushes you against a rational sense of self preservation. It makes no sense, but seems to have a sense of truth to it. The need to step out into that void is not even a conscious thought but there you are stepping closer and closer.

Apparently, approximately half of us suffer or experience this 'call of the void' or 'l'appel du vide' as it is commonly known.

Researchers call it by the only slightly more technical term, 'High Place Phenomenon' or HPP. Many of these psychologists and scientists tell us this is not necessarily a suicidal tendency, and probably nothing to worry about, nor read too much into, it is merely mental interference, a warning sign overlaid with intuition that only for a brief moment confuses us because it is actually a realisation of danger.[2]

It feels like something beyond us, a dizzying compulsion and beckoning of some form of truth. This 'call of the void' is more likely to be a deeper expression and compulsion of our nature as human beings, our natural will as free independent beings; a reminder of our ultimate control over our own life.

Our contemporary lives are hemmed in and overwhelmed by controlling limitations and expectations. We are constantly assured and reminded of our privileged freedoms, but our life feels 'free-less', we are imprisoned by endless pressures, constraints and ironically by a multitude of opportunity.

The seemingly vast individual opportunities and expectations of contemporary life bring the demand that we each define anew who we are, that our identity itself together with all the associated opportunity found and lost, is our own individual responsibility, is an existential weight difficult to bear, and from which we turn and seek escape through any distraction or self-deception we can find.

But one thing we can do, one simple act under our control and ours alone, is our actual life. If we choose, we can fling ourselves into the void, escape at last, and float into the sky, away from weight, pressure and expectation; the most simple, pure and poetic expression of our individual freedom.

The child, only too aware of its complete dependence, its life restricted beyond belief, tires of the constant control, crawls over to the open apartment window, looks back, mischievously at its carers and with a giggle throws itself out; take that, I am human too, I am as free as you.

The depressed, oppressed, alienated modern individual, diagnosed and treated, medicated and processed, barely hanging on to any social connection, misunderstood and silenced, digs a pen or blade into their arm in a series of evenly spaced red lines in a satisfying confirmation of their presence, their identity; they are not an entirely powerless human being, they are as good as you.

2 Several research papers on High Place Phenomenon (HHP) have been published including the Florida State University study which concluded: "...individuals who report experiencing the phenomenon are not necessarily suicidal; rather, the experience of HPP may reflect their sensitivity to internal cues and actually affirm their will to live." Extract from 'An urge to jump affirms the urge to live: an empirical examination of the high place phenomenon', Jennifer L Hames 1 , Jessica D Ribeiro, April R Smith, Thomas E Joiner Jr, Florida State University, Department of Psychology, 2012 Feb;136(3):1114-20. doi: 10.1016/j.jad.2011.10.035. Epub 2011 Nov 25 PMID: 22119089 DOI: 10.1016/j.jad.2011.10.035
See also:
High place phenomenon: prevalence and clinical correlates in two German samples, Teismann T, Brailovskaia J, Schaumburg S, Wannemüller A., BMC Psychiatry. 2020 Sep 30;20(1):478. doi: 10.1186/s12888-020-02875-8. PMID: 32998717.

28 Edge of the parapet, Shanghai.

At a broad social level, we can perhaps recognise this phenomenon in grand collective acts of identity that seem to contradict self-interest. Screams of resistance and assertion of freedom from those politically alienated and placated by people who know best and infuriatingly and patronisingly, do know our best interest; thereby robbing us of even our own knowing. The only voice that will be heard is the one that hurts, makes no sense and finally gets attention, to hell with the consequences.

Sometime perhaps this assertion of freedom is more important than the self-harm it causes, this cry of independence, this scream of identity; as free and human. Perhaps a proof of ultimate responsibility, an assertion of independence, is worth it, is more important than survival or at least a step closer to knowing you are still you, still free.

Perhaps 'l'appel du vide' is a reminder of this human essentiality; a reminder that a true life is one spent with one foot out the door.

The architect then, weighed down and disempowered by unreasonable demands, regulations, committees and contracts; intense pressures of costs, time and construction processes; vested interest, opinion, consultation and good taste, is largely silenced on issues of substance and all too often relegated to the creative generation of competitive marketable images for... well, Instagram.

How shocking then would it really be if the architect was drawn too near the edge, took that final inviting step out over the scaffold and fell.

What if the fall through the not-so-clean air was also a fall through the web of impediments and distortions to the true mission of the architect? A realisation not to rise high in jungles of glass steel and concrete to continue a destructive obsession with height in an ill-founded escape from the ground of our earth, but a reminder to look down, and understand that the architect's mission is to connect us more deeply with the nature of the ground from which we all belong, and long to return. The beckoning of a neglected earth from which we have risen so high, is an invitation for us to rediscover an interconnection with the ground, within the natural world from which we have alienated ourselves, to find our place within it and restore a symbiotic interdependence with nature.

This seemingly irresistible attraction of the architect to the edge, drawing us down and beckoning us to step out and be reunited again with the ground, the 'l'appel du vide', might also be the call of architecture; a call for us to be true to the nature of architecture, and ultimately true to our own nature.

What matters then, if the ultimate enlightenment from this fall of the architect is hitting the ground? Paradoxically, the survival of architecture may depend on this return to earth.

True and Not True: The Architecture of Nothing

The paradox of science is that its success in understanding nature has created problems for its understanding of human nature...Whereas the prescientific world viewed the universe as full of purpose and desire, the scientific revolution transformed nature into an inert, mindless entity.

Kenan Malik, *Materialism, Mechanism and the Human Mind* (2001) [1]

1 Kenan Malik, *Materialism, Mechanism and the Human Mind, New Humanist*, 116.3, 2001.

29 Laminated timber grid shell
structure of Bunjil Place, a community
performing arts, gallery and library in
Narre Warren, Victoria, Australia by
fjmtstudio.

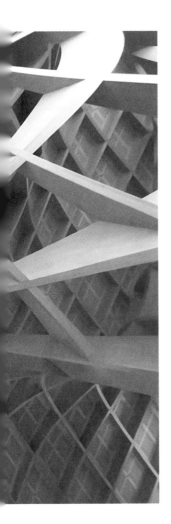

The law of non-contravalence or non-contradiction, has been such a staple of our western thought and logic, that it seems hard to think outside its boundaries. The principal or law of non-contravalence is one of our three fundamentals of logic[2] and has been a foundation upon which our scientific inquiry, reasoning and communication are built.

How can something possibility be true and at the same time, not true?

Such logical foundations and seemingly self-evident truths are perhaps not as firm and solid as they first appear. The law of non-contravalence, at least to some extent, is tripped up or trapped by paradox that freezes our established logic. Despite the contradiction, we feel some kind of truth in paradox, a truth that is hard to explain or communicate within the limitations of our language and classical logic. Paradox is not merely a clever manipulation of language, it is a proposition that seems contradictory, but when investigated, when taking the journey through paradox, it seems to reveal some kind of truth. The liar paradox; 'this sentence is a lie,' [3] is perhaps the most famous example of a trap that seems to reveal the limitation of non-contraction.

Perhaps more profound is the paradox of Quantum Mechanics. The superposition of states that quantum particles can theoretically exist in at the same time, provokes and seemingly challenges non-contravalences.

The physicist Erwin Schrödinger devised a now famous thought experiment that illustrated or challenged the apparent paradox of quantum superposition: A cat is in a box, its life is dependent on a potential single atom decay that would trigger the release of poison. According to the Copenhagen interpretation of quantum mechanics, after a while the cat is both alive and not alive; until the superposition ends with the opening of the box by an observer.[4] Until the atom collapses from non-decay/decay the cat is suspended; alive and not alive, both possible, both true. It is the dependence on and release by the action of the observer that resolves and ends this dual simultaneity, but within the box is there really a cat both alive and not alive, or merely the possibility of either/both?

2 The three laws of western 'Aristotelian logic' and rationality include the law of identity, law of non-contradiction or non-contravanence and the law of the excluded middle.

3 A hallmark of classical logic 'This sentence is a lie' is paradoxical as it seems to be a statement from a liar but if the statement is true then it cannot be a lie; if on the other hand, the liar is telling a lie, the statement is true and not a lie—a kind of continuous circular contradiction.

4 One can even set up quite ridiculous cases. A cat is penned up in a steel chamber, along with the following device (which must be secured against direct interference by the cat): in a Geiger counter, there is a tiny bit of radioactive substance, so small, that perhaps in the course of the hour one of the atoms decays, but also, with equal probability, perhaps none; if it happens, the counter tube discharges and through a relay releases a hammer that shatters a small flask of hydrocyanic acid. If one has left this entire system to itself for an hour, one would say that the cat still lives if meanwhile no atom has decayed. The first atomic decay would have poisoned it. The psi-function of the entire system would express this by having in it the living and dead cat (pardon the expression) mixed or smeared out in equal parts. It is typical of these cases that an inde-terminacy originally restricted to the atomic domain becomes transformed into macroscopic indeterminacy, which can then be resolved by direct observation. That prevents us from so naïvely accepting as valid a "blurred model" for representing reality. In itself, it would not embody anything unclear or contradictory.
Erwin Schrödinger, *Die gegenwärtige Situation in der Quantenmechanik (The present situation in quantum mechanics)*, Naturwissenschaften. 23 (48): 807–812, 1935.

5 There is an extended history of dialetheian thought and in contemporary work, Graham Priest makes the case of Dialethesism as an advancement and extension of human comprehension and knowledge. Graham Priest, *In Contra-diction*, Dordrecht: Martinus Nijhoff, 1987. Graham Priest, *The Logic of Buddhist Philosophy goes Beyond True and False*, Comparative Philosophy Volume 1, No. 2 (2010): 24-54.

6 Gestalt psychology was founded by Max Wertheimer, Wolfgang Köhler, and Kurt Koffka through a series of works between 1915-1935. Gestalt principles of visual perception include proximity, similarity, figure-ground, continuity, closure, and connection.

Schrödinger was illustrating the absurd misconception of superposition of states, but his apparent paradox captured our collective imagination and illustrates both our difficulty in acceptance and non-acceptance of contradiction.

Challenges to the law of non-contravalence and forms of acceptance of contradiction have both an extended history and currency. Accepting the possibility of 'true contradictions', or that there can be true statements that are also not true, is known as Dialetheism (Greek δι- di-'twice' and ἀλήθεια alḗtheia-true).[5] Dialetheists can accept some forms of contradictions and perhaps escape and accommodate the dilemma of paradoxical 'truth'.

But can 'true' and 'not true' really be held together in the same moment?

The insightful, empathetic and imaginative experience of the human child has little problem with this contrava-lence. Their world is full of simultaneity, and truth is as yet unencumbered and distorted by singularity, exclu-sion and lies. Nothing encumbers the child, nothing separates the child from the world and the extended life around it; they coexist in the same spaces, places and moments.

There is insight in the non-separational experience of the child worlds, and also within the paradoxical nature of the use of 'nothing' to define this non-separation of human innocence with place. When we say nothing separates the child from the natural world what are we saying, that 'no' 'thing' separates us or 'nothing' sepa-rates? When we think of 'nothing' what are we thinking of? Is it 'no-thing'; a pure description of complete absence of 'things', or is it possible for nothing to be a noun 'Nothing' and thereby possess some dimension of thingness? There is a paradox to nothing, it is the 'no thing' between that thereby joins, and the 'Nothing' that is in between us; it is both separation and connection.

Nothing as a noun, as the identifier, is familiar to architects. It is in some ways how architects see through to the nature and depth of architecture.

30 Rubin's vase (sometimes known as the Rubin face or the Figure-ground vase) is a famous set of cognitive optical illusions developed around 1915 by the Danish psychologist Edgar Rubin.

Architects must learn to see the void as well as the solid, the ground as well as the figure and to be able to invert these. Understanding of the interrelationship of figure and ground, solid and void, poché and space has a long history in architecture; including at an urban scale, as seen in the influential 1748 plans of Rome by Giambattista Nolli, but the concept of figure/ground perception developed out of early twentieth-century Gestalt psychology.[6] 'Gestalt' theory, from the German meaning 'form' or 'shape', suggests that we group distinct elements of perception in our experience of the world and combine them into a greater, more meaningful whole.

We all seem to privilege the solid, the figure over the background. It is an innate human perception, essential to a child's ability to organise and group the objects of the world around them. But most people can easily see the void when it is shown to them, and then switch back and forth, even hold both simultaneous and still in our gaze; hold both true and not true at the same moment.

When the solid is the dominant, and becomes the field or ground, then it is the absence of matter; the void, or hole, that becomes the figure.

31 Cave in Juukan Gorge, Hammersley Ranges, Western Australia. This sacred cave site contained evidence of 46,000 year old direct link to the ancestors of Puutu Kunti Kurrama and Pinikura traditional owners living today. The caves were destroyed in the expansion of an iron ore mine, in 2020.

In this instance the 'Nothing', rather than 'no thing', becomes the giver of identity.

Holes in the earth for example, or holes in some of our manufactured products, such as donuts, bagels or peppermints, have the precedence of identity. The hole or 'Nothing' becomes the bearer of identity.[7]

The cave is another example, and perhaps the most essential and defining for architecture. This is a foundational archetype of human habitation; of safety, shelter and retreat. It is the figure and void of architecture in a hostile, hard world of matter.

If it is the void, the space, the hole, the 'Nothing' that is the essence and identity of architecture, that not only supports human inhabitation, but identity; then perhaps we should focus our attention on the essential matter that defines this essence, the surface definition of this space. We could then reduce this defining and identity-giving surface to a material minimum, reduce it to its essential matter. It is then the role of the solid, the matter, the mass to form and define the space and identity of inhabitation; of architecture.

7 Suki Finn, edited by Nigel Warburton, *Is a hole a real thing, or just a place where something isn't?* aeon, <https://aeon.co/ ideas/is-a-hole-a-real-thing-or-just-a- place-where-something-isnt>, 2018.

32 Students of Ball State University with Professors Gernot Riether and Andrew Wit, Underwood Pavilion Parametric tensegrity structure, Indiana, USA, 2014.

Perhaps we could consider the evolution of architecture in terms of a reduction or refinement to the minimum essential mass of definition: An architectural evolution from a void/cave, discovered or carved out of the great matter of the earth, though the numerous technological advancements of assembly and construction; to a minimum of mass and surface for the definition and enclosure of space and void; an evolution from weight to lightness; an architecture of minimum structure, mass, material and weight; that can define a space of our inhabitation and social identity.

Lightweight architecture of minimum material weight will develop structures where the ratio between the dead load (the weight of the structure) and the live load (the weight of the use and environmental condition) are as low as possible. We think of membrane, shell, cabled and folded structural enclosure systems.

These lightweight systems would seem to be true to this moment of environmental crisis, as they use a minimum of material, and their lightness of footprint projects an appropriate sensitivity or reduced intervention on the earth.

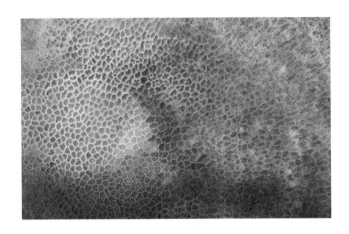

33 Close-up yellow-red colors texture of a fossilised sea sponge with a cellular structure.

Such lightness in material is usually offset by an increased labour and technical expertise over more weighty and less precise constructions. While this clearly has a cost implication, we have to ask ourselves if increased labour is actually preferable at this moment of employment stress and social inequity, particularly when compared to the wholistic environmental and social cost of mining material weight from the earth and transporting it across the globe.

The life of the natural world is a rich source of models for lightweight forms of support and enclosure.

Perhaps the most foundational of these forms is the *Pneus*; internally pressurised envelope forms. It is the cellar structure of life, internally stabilised, remarkably adaptable and reproducible into a vast array of extended and geometric systems of enclosure.

Shell forms, on the other hand, derive their strength from geometric and spatial continuity. They can be continuous in the form of double curved thin surfaces between stiffened ribs or more open interconnected geometric forms of extreme lightness. These surface systems can be extended into exclusively tensile structures to form webs that depend on connections and geometric continuity to create remarkably adaptable and minimal material form in relation to strength.

8 Michael Hensel and Achim Menges, *Morpho-Ecologies* p.21, Chapter: Morpho-Ecologies: Towards an inclusive Discourse of Heterogeneous Space, AA Publications, 2006.

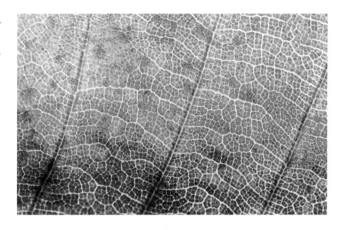

34 Leaf structure, magnified image.

The skeletal systems of lifeforms have both interlocking arched rib and flexible joints that allow for remarkable flexibility and mobility, and also the tetravalent layered three-dimensional grid of the bones themselves, giving directional strength and lightness, at its most optimised perhaps in the natural structure of flight.

Perhaps the most direct, influential, integrated and relatable lightweight structure is the progressive lightness, rise and enclosure of a tree. At the core is the compression of pneumatic cells that harden into tampering curvilinear forms of cantilever, grounded into the earth through tensile anchors, and forming a shade shelter and enclosure through the responsive ribbed shell-like surfaces of the leaf.

Biomimicry, an extension of the form of natural systems into our constructions, has been, in many ways, present from the birth of classical architecture, generally in the weighty forms of bearing wood and stone; lintel and beam.

We now can renew this 'turn to nature', but in a purer search for lightness; for a minimum weight of material. The Morpho-Ecologies research work of Michael Hensel and Achim Menges seeks to distill the process of form generation to essential and 'natural' parametrics.'to achieve morphological complexity and performance capacity in material constituents without separating formation from materialisation'. [8]

35 fjmtstudio, Sun-shading system in the library at the University of Technolgy Sydney. The central leaf life shade rotates to open and close in relation to the position of the sun.

Perhaps such turns to more natural, organic, fluid, lighter form and structure could be a contrast with, and even atonement for, the heavy destructive Cartesian imprints of our settlements.

Perhaps also, in our turn to biophilic, biomorphic design and deeper connections to nature, we can glance far back through the heavy imposition of colonial ordering and domination of the natural landscape and its original human custodians; and see some form of connection and empathy for a lightness born from an unshakeable interconnection with the natural world and the forms of all its life.

Perhaps too, we can accept some transgression, at certain moments, of the law of non-contravalence and our tight embrace of the binary of true and false. We may accept perhaps, that the natural world is not always so emphatic, that a blurring between these binary poles may help us to see more clearly and broadly, to see true and also not true.

The boundaries we draw through the landscape, and indeed those that define our own social and individual identity, are not always so clear, so determined; they are blurred, changeable, ambiguous, open and full of simultaneity.

The boundaries of place, for example, are indistinct and multidimensional, as much defined by the natural figuring of landscape as the imprints and stories of human events. Landscape edges, rivers and gullies; life, stories and memories; all separate and join us at the same time, while always in constant change and transformation.

The imposition of a fence or a wall to introduce a clarifying non-contravalence into this dialetheia is an act of transgression, an imposition, that attempts to deny the elusive and fluid nature of life and landscape; human identity and place. It is not possible to understand our interrelationship with the natural landscape, nor to find and reconcile our place in our world, without some form of acceptance of dialetheia. We have to be able to suspend our unconditional belief in the binary of non-contravalence; our western foundation of logic, and accept that, at moments, true and not true is possible, insightful and revealing and is an essential part of nature, and our nature.

The Consciousness
of the Architect

If you think of Brick, you say to Brick, 'What do you want, Brick?' And Brick says to you, 'I like an Arch.' And if you say to Brick, 'Look, arches are expensive, and I can use a concrete lintel over you. What do you think of that, Brick?' Brick says, 'I like an Arch.' And it's important, you see, that you honor the material that you use. [..] You can only do it if you honor the brick and glorify the brick instead of shortchanging it.

Louis Kahn [1]

1 Louis Kahn, Transcribed from the 2003 documentary *My Architect: A Son's Journey by Nathaniel Kahn*, Master class at Penn, 1971.

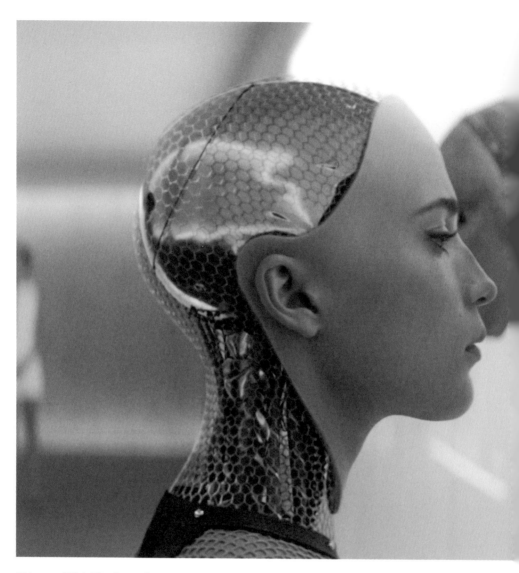

36 A scene of Alicia Vikander as robot Ava touching Sonoya Mizuno as robot Kyoko lips in Alex Garland's *Ex Machina*, 2014.

Consciousness has long been something of a blind spot in our science, hard to deny but easy to ignore; hard to explain, easy to intuit.

In recent years we have seen a renewed focus on how consciousness can be explained and how central it may be to our understanding of our world and the nature of our existence.

Perhaps there is also a sense of urgency in understanding consciousness beyond a mere human consciousness as we try to come to terms with the ethical and environmental issues of our time. As we try to understand how we value forms of life or even define life, extending it not only to the breath of the natural world and natural systems but our own transformations of our world in the form of our inventions, automations, manufacturings and particularly in the form of Artificial Intelligence. These are all pressing our limited definitions of consciousness. We are searching for tools and instruments to navigate our way through territory where our sight is weak but the land full of crevices.

There are some important and challenging concepts that may help guide us through this territory. One of the most challenging and difficult for us to grasp is panpsychism, a term from the Greek *pan*-everything or whole and *psyche*-mind/soul. This is the concept that consciousness is not exclusively a human or animal attribute but it is present in all things. Sentience, in some form, is ubiquitous, exists throughout the natural world and in all our human re-workings of this world.

This is a concept that stands in contrast with modern scientific materialism which has informed so much of our effective and efficient understanding of the world and has in many ways got us where we are today, for good and perhaps ill. Nevertheless, panpsychism has a long history in human thought, from Plato's entire world as a 'living being endowed with soul and intelligence,' Spinoza's monism, Schopenhauer's extension of 'inner essence' and a rich line of modern thinking.

2 David Chalmers, *Facing up to the problem of Consciousness*, pp. 577-588, Journal of Consciousness Studies Vol. 2, No. 3, pp. 200-219, Imprint Academic, 1995.

In more recent times the Australian philosopher David Chalmers has suggested that it is a potential response to what he has termed the 'hard problem of consciousness', the mystery of awareness that seems to underpin our experience of the world.[2]

But it remains a challenging concept as it seems to question not only our scientific materialism, which has little purpose for the immateriality of conscious souls, but also our Judeo-Christian tradition that preferences the souls of humanity above all other forms of animal and natural life, which are to be served up for human 'use'.

Rather than separate ourselves from nature, objectifying it for instrumental use, an environmental philosophy of empathy that extends sentience deep into the natural world, in many ways supported by indigenous thought, is more intuitive and natural to our own sense of being; it is surely the natural insight of our children.

This same insight is central to the art and nature of the craft of architecture, and it is hardly surprising therefore that all children are architects. Every child intuitively knows what it takes us years to re-teach them as adults, to see the life in making. Architecture is the giving of life to building or perhaps more accurately the uncovering of life in the transformation of a site.

This recognition of consciousness extension is inherent in the very creative act. When we design with empathy and sincerity it is not a wilful act of determination but a discovery and following of a life outside our own. We may launch a project with a sense of direction or aspiration but must quickly then get in the boat and accept the course it sets for us, follow its nature and path. This is the 'flow', the acceptance that the creative act is not our agency but exercised through us.

As architects, we are used to thinking about consciousness within architecture, of finding a form that embodies social purpose and aspirations, of imbuing of architecture with life. Even simple material units architects imbue with life or mind.

37 Ancient Theatre of Taormina, Sicily, Italy, built in the third century BC.

Take for instance the most basic unit of construction, the brick, pressed and moulded from the earth and clay on which we stand. Its properties and dimensions are determined in relation to our own bodies, and our ability to hold its weight and proportions in one hand. We form this unit, assemble it into enclosures and walls and then at some point step back and ponder its nature and intent, perhaps even its life and ambitions. Louis Kahn famously asked, 'what does a brick want to be?' Is this the moment when the builder becomes an architect, when we see the life and consciousness beyond our own designer wilfulness?

And if this is the insight that makes us architects, the insight of a child re-learned, how is it lost so easily? Is it simply when we forget to ask the question anew on each and every project; as we gradually come to believe that there is no question to be asked; consciousness receding back to only us, only me and my will; observing only an object with no material depth or life of its own?

3 Oscar Wilde, 'Lady Windermere's Fan', A Play about a Good Woman, Third Act, first produced at the St James's Theatre in London,1892.

Is this when the architect falls and becomes merely a conjurer of images? When we fail to see the nature of the brick and the transcendence of form and we are merely beguiled by the shape and passing popularity of the arch.

How could we forsake the insight at the very heart of our profession and our art? Perhaps it is like the inevitable loss of innocence of a child, as the true nature of the world is buried in the struggle for identity, self-assertiveness, worldliness and cynicism. The contemporary architect is similarly buried under the proliferation of images, the reductive speed and processes of production and the exploitative commodification of our work. Architecture reduced to consumer object; thin and passing in its appeal, interest and use.

The immeasurable is overwhelmed by the measurable, and we seem to know the price of everything and the value of nothing.[3] Where once we saw life, we now see only use.

So, in returning to the brick, if we are interested in it beyond a mere instrumental use, if we are curious about its nature and think it may have some form of consciousness, we should be cautious in our use of the arch.

If Kahn was right and the arch is the ultimate aspiration of the brick, then it is a most honourable and transcendental form. But it is not ours, it is beyond our wilfulness and belongs only to the brick. So, we should be sure to ask the question again, and make sure this is the time and place for the brick, and if so, ask what form it wishes to take in this particular moment.

38 Louis Kahn, Indian Institute of
Management, Ahmedabad, India,
1974.

The Fencing of Architecture and the Villa of the Architect

The first person who, having enclosed a plot of land, took it into his head to say this is mine and found people simple enough to believe him was the true founder of civil society. What crimes, wars, murders, what miseries and horrors would the human race have been spared, had someone pulled up the stakes or filled in the ditch and cried out to his fellow men: 'Do not listen to this imposter. You are lost if you forget the fruits of the earth belong to all and the earth to no one!.

Jean-Jacques Rousseau, *The Social Contract* (1913) [1]

1 Jean-Jacques Rousseau, translated with introduction by G.D. H. Cole, edited by Ernest Rhys, *The Social Contract and Discourses*, London and Toronto: J.M. Dent and Sons, 1923.

39 Sturt National Park, a section of
the Dingo Fence that stretches across
5,600km and three Australian states.

Perhaps the two most destructive architectural typologies we have developed are the fence and the villa. They have (dis)figured land settlement in a way that has partitioned and controlled the landscape for exploitation, driving human alienation, inequality and environmental degradation on a now breathtaking scale.

The Fence

The wall is a device of defence and protection; from the hostilities of nature and our fellow human being. Its efficacy depends on its strength, height, weight and depth. Our settlements over the ages evidence the projection and defence of social power and authority through the walls that enclose them and localise concentrations of authority.

A shortening from the term defence, 'fens' is the fourteenth century origin of the word fence. The fence is a distillation of the wall. Perhaps an effective restraint to animal life, but as actual physical protection to natural and human hostilities it is weak and next to useless. Its power is not physical at all; it is symbolic and representational; it is a marker of an invisible force. Fences represent boundaries that will be enforced.

As common feudal fields gave way to legal servitudes, fences defined and partitioned the land for individual private use, or they represented the invasive claiming of land from nature and its human custodians during western colonisation and oppression of First Nation/Indigenous Peoples, fencing that would be subsequently strengthened with governmental laws and policies. The fencing of land was a quick, economical and efficient instrument of private ownership, power and the associated exclusion. Moreover, in its unequivocal statement of ownership, it serves up this land for independent private purpose and environmental exploitation. The fence has been a remarkable instrument of occupation, control and suspect claims of ownership. We are so conditioned and intimidated by its insidious power and force, that we seem so easily deterred from otherwise entirely rational paths of transgression.

The Villa

The villa occupies a special place in the history of western architecture, in particular during the Renaissance and Modern period.

The idea of a dwelling away from the city, away from the village, away from society, isolated in a more natural landscape, was a compelling proposition for the wealthy. It offered a withdrawal and a sense of greater communion with nature. But this was a very privileged, mannered and rarified form of communion. This was not a farmhouse or working communion with the landscape where the ground was figured and shaped for agrarian production and likewise the dwelling was figured by the landscape. The villa was to command the landscape, its force and even geometry radiating from its central high ground position, extending the vision and influence of the inhabitant.

The form of the villa was perhaps at its most idealised in the work of the Italian Renaissance architect Andrea Palladio and in particular with the Villa Rotonda which epitomised this ideal in a centralised temple-like form. Sited on the high point of the landscape and raised on a podium, its porticos and rooms give commanding views over the manicured landscape of lawns, meadows and trees, with the city of Vicenza on the distant horizon. A perfection of mathematical composition, balanced symmetry and form, this villa controls and spatially defines a transformed natural landscape.

In the twentieth-century the modernist villa continued its typological command of the land. The contrasting interrelation between landscape and object form was further reinforced as the landscape was released from geometric manicuration, and the literal surveillance of this 'untouched' landscape increased through continuous strip windows and fully glazed walls.

The pure expressions of this continuity and adaptation are epitomised in Le Corbusier's exquisite Villa Savoye of 1929, which was raised up on piloti so the piano nobile could survey the landscape through continuous and defensible strip windows; easy to look out, but more difficult to see the surveyor.

Or perhaps, it was most clear in Mies van der Rohe's poetic, lightness of touch on the landscape with the Farnsworth House. The irony of this almost transcendental suspended villa lies in the commanding nature of its absolute transparency, which demands ownership, control and privacy over its extended landscape site. Completed in 1951, the villa is carefully sited within twenty-four hectares of beautiful grassland and forest landscape next to the Fox River in Illinois. This singular special villa is comprised of two suspended planes of floor and wall, with a solid services module replacing the Palladian central room, so that the occupant is constantly projected out to the landscape through a continuous glazed perimeter. All seeing and being seen, this extraordinary and beautiful villa is a perfect expression of the social withdrawal of the wealthy into an extended privatised landscape, where it is both the overlooking and the dismissive visibility of the occupant that make clear the location of power and control of the landscape.

The villa is unimaginable without categoric and excessive private property ownership. It epitomises the power of the wealthy individual, a power over the landscape, to control, command it, bend it to will and monitor it through literal and phenomenological surveillance.

41 Mies van der Rohe, Farnsworth House, Fox River, Plano, Illinois, 1946-50.

Architect

The isolation of the site and the wealthy patron nature of the villa owner set the ideal tabula rasa for the formal and spatial experiments of the architect. Here, freed from the constraints of social settlement and budgetary limitations, the architect could innovate, challenge and test; explore concepts and ideas that may be prototypes for future projects and even new directions in architecture. But is there not something Faustian about such notions? What kind of prototype is suggested by such an extreme social and environmental context, and what of the inherently destructive and unsustainable social and environmental nature of the project of the private villa? Irrespective of their individual brilliance and beauty, what use are such indulgent prototypes?

Suburb

These two typologies of villa and fence, combined in a tragically compressed hybrid to create the most destructive form of land settlement the world has witnessed; the suburban dwelling. The 'landscape' setting for the villa was reduced to about 550 sqm with its desired isolation and independence entirely dependent on perimeter fencing. Perhaps if you were to squint enough you may be able to see the evolution of Palladio's idealised villas or maybe even shades of the Farnsworth House if the suburb was exclusive enough.

This distorted, idealised form of modern private property ownership, independence and control, extended like a virus. Fuelled by the motorcar and freeway, the suburb of miniature idealised villas flattened natural landscapes into placeless sameness and extended urbanisation in a ridiculously disproportionate ratio of population increase to land consumption and utilisation.

2 Aldof Loos, 'Architektur', Der Sturm 15, Vienna, 1910.

The consequences of this virus have been environmental destruction on a stunning scale: loss of wildlife habitat, temperature increases as urban heat island effects are extended, urban runoff and flooding, excessive and needless energy consumption, pollution and more per capita carbon emissions than any other form of settlement. Meanwhile, the human psychological cost of such fenced isolation and loss of community further feeds our alienation and helplessness.

Notwithstanding the inherent self-destructive nature of this typology, perhaps it is not surprising that in the wealthy suburbs, the villa continues to be a focus for architects. The attraction of the independent patron, sense of isolation and separation for experimentation seems too difficult to resist, irrespective of the illusionary and damaging nature of this isolation.

Does it matter if the villa is the work of a good or bad architect, given the tragic consequence of an enamour with this infectious, destructive and all-consuming typology?

May I lead you to the shores of a mountain lake? The sky is blue, the water green and everything is profoundly peaceful. Mountains and clouds are reflected in the lake, and so are houses, farmyards, courtyards and chapels. They do not seem man-made, but more like the product of God's workshop, like the mountains and trees, the clouds and the blue sky. And everything breathes beauty and tranquillity.

Ah, what is that? A false note in this harmony. Like an unwelcome scream. In the centre, beneath the peasants' homes which were created not by them, but by God, stands a villa: Is it the product of a good or a bad architect? I do not know, I only know that peace, tranquillity and beauty are no more. Why does the architect both good and bad violate the lake...

Aldof Loos (1910) [2]

The Search for the Universal in the Placelessness of the Architect

I take a seat on the bus. I am late. I am behind in my work. My family needs more time from me. I am surrounded by silent, blank, tired faces and advertising, the ceaseless noise of the city and the noise of the bus. The seat is uncomfortable. This bus, this day and this city is like all the others. Endless, alienating and placeless. I am struggling under the burden of everyday existence.

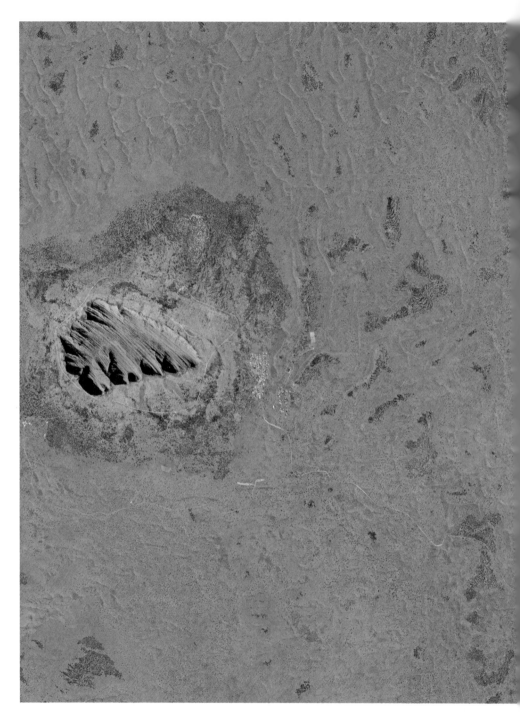

43 Uluru, Kata Tjuta National Park,
NT Australia. The Yankunytjatjara and
Pitjantjatjara People or Anangu have
been custodians of this land for over
30,000 years.

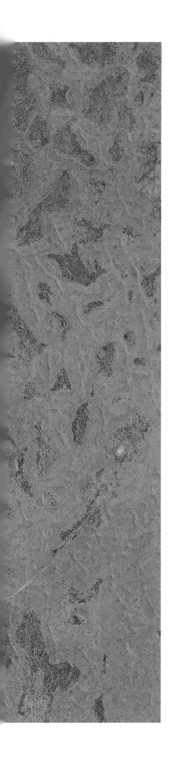

Authentic contemporary connection to place is deeply problematic.

The sense of interconnected inhabitation, developed through centuries of close and intimate settlement with the land and our ancestors, was lost with the embrace of modernity and all it offered. We were absorbed with the great rewards that modernity could bring to our lives, but at the same time, there remained a sense of melancholic loss for what could not be regained.

Modernity offered us the entire world, an extraordinary expanse of technological possibilities and freedom but left us with a sense of perpetual displacement. It seems only tenuous connections can be made within the speed, breadth and sweep of modernity. We are left with a sense of homelessness, a longing for interconnection and a place in the world, a longing a for a sense of community, and the inseparable cultural bonds that grounds us.

The grounded pre-modern connection to a specific locale, place and culture interwoven within the specific has been displaced and lost. This is the reality of our contemporary condition from which we cannot escape, but inwardly we long for a return. This longing and loss provoke two reactions, a superficial turning back at the wake of loss in the form of nostalgia, or a blind denial in the form of an obsession with the new, with the Zeitgeist.

Nostalgia and the Zeitgeist are about time; two opposite poles, perhaps, of an attitude to time, but in fact closer together than first appears. Nostalgia (so beloved by the conservatives) and the Zeitgeist (so frequently the catch-cry of the avant-garde) are both a resistance to time—to the flowing, equalizing, continuous motion of moments and events that is time. One wants desperately to remember what is already lost, longs for the security of the past, for what is familiar, comfortable and seemed forever true. The other wants to forget, fight, and resist the pull of the past, thinking that it itself will never become past.

The grounded sentimentality of nostalgia and the shining light of the Zeitgeist.

1 Louis Kahn, ed. Paul Zucker, *Monumentality*, in *New Architecture and City Planning*, pp. 577-588, New York: Philosophical Library, 1999.

2 Ibid.

So-called 'architectural heritage' often struggles under the weight of nostalgia; it turns its back, hoping it can forever resist time, go back and restore what has been compromised or damaged. It seeks an understandable comfort and meaning in our history, what we knew and now idealise and miss, it wants to restore or recreate, or at least reference the past somehow, grasping at a lost sense of continuity and connection.

Nostalgia's disaffected twin, Zeitgeist is equally defined by the past, but a rejection and resentment of the past. It is the heroic mission of the avant-garde to only look forward, reject the weight and pull of heritage, and value the new as a rejection of failed preceding generations.

Is there a meaningful difference between these two possibilities? Is there really a political dimension to what is behind these terms, beyond that of the familiar maintenance and updating of syntax that is essential to our free-market consumer culture and political slumber? Are these both merely futile compensations or distractions from our deeper placelessness and lost sense of meaningful interconnection with our world?

Perhaps our escape is possible through neither turning back, nor running away, but standing and accepting. Perhaps we can seek a path through a more abstract and universal sense of interconnection. Not the specific connections of a lost pre-modern culture, but the more difficult connection of the universal; an authentic modern interconnection with a world which is individual, but common to us all, direct and unmediated by the conditioning of the specific.

At the close of World War II Louis Kahn, in an essay entitled '*Monumentality*', attempted to map out the direction for twentieth-century architecture. He wrote enthusiastically of the possibilities provided by new technology and new science, "of living in an unbalanced state of relativity."[1] Kahn was excited at the new structural possibilities, the new social programs, and the new monumentality of continuous structures, much as we are today excited by the possibilities of prefabrication and modularisation, 5D building integrated modelling, augmented reality technology, artificial intelligence, robotics and advanced analytics;

to remake our world and address global urbanisation and climate change.

But in this excitement and simplification, Kahn pointed out the enigmatic nature of monumentality, suggesting that it cannot be intentionally created and that it is more about content than form:

Neither the finest material nor the most advanced technology need enter a work of monumental character for the same reason that the finest ink was not required to draw up the Magna Carta.[2]

The character and content to which Kahn refers have both a spiritual and social dimension, and it is perhaps not so much what is changing in humanity, as what is unchanging that is the subject of monumentality.

Of course, temporal human values, deeds, and the glorification of individuals will continue to be the subject of architecture attempting to represent and monumentalise. But if we untangle the showy images, the branding and the attention seeking, we realise that the quality that remains, that continues to have meaning for us, has nothing to do with any individual, with the ego of the patron or the architect.

Monumentality is concerned not with private interest, but with what is shared—the public interest, the willing sacrifice of the interests of the individual for the collective. These are the values and content to be embodied and represented in our public institutions, in a monumental architecture. But equally, it is concerned with what is outside any temporal human institution and seeks a spiritual connection to something fundamental in our humanity, something eternal.

With the development of a contemporary sense of universal connection with the world, it may be possible to begin a form of authentic re-connection to the specific and to a locale. These connections will be subtle, as our modern condition is one of displacement and our interconnection is primarily universal, but this does not make it less profound, and perhaps ultimately makes it more so, as it is free from the myth and distortion of socio-religious culture.

The universal is the basic shared phenomenological human condition of being together on this earth, framed and orientated through landscape and architecture. Experience and interpretation of the reality of this basic condition can ground us within the flux and noise of contemporary placelessness.

Perhaps an authentic architecture can begin through restating and interpreting this condition; making metaphorical connections to our shared phenomenological condition and framing our relation with the world. Abstract relations that simultaneously project forward through form and technology to reframe our relation to the world, and at the same time, reach back to connect us to what is unchanging in our world.

Irrespective of the specifics of our culture, the basic existential condition of being in our world, is shared, we all exist together on the earth and under the sky; between groundplane and skyplane. We carve and dig into the ground, piling up the earth and clay. We reach up with posts and frames, stretch and weave glass and fabric in canopies and vaults. We shape and figure the space between the plane of the sky and the plane of the ground, distorting both in an attempt to secure our place.

In architecture, representations of reality are postulated and explored through the formal relations of the building and the reality of its making. Not the surface application of an idealised image, but through the spatial organisation, formal order, structure, construction and specific relation with the site and interpretation of the programme. Thus, the representational nature or meaning in architecture does not depend on its stability, function or, the efficiency of the means of its production, but on the way in which all of these have been limited and subordinated or transformed by purely formal requirements. The purpose is therefore not a restrictive condition that compromises our art, but an integral element of specific representation.

Architectural representation becomes the making of critical frames through which to understand our experience of the world; a formal means of cognitive effect with an ethical and social purpose.

142

44 Erik Gunnar Asplund, Woodland
Cemetery Chapel, Stockholm,
Sweden, 1918.

But it is also important to understand the limits of this
representation. The architectural framings of the world
are not, for example, political and never will be. This is
beyond the limits of architecture. They only frame the
events that occur around them and which are staged
within them, accommodating comedy and tragedy with
equal indifference.

However, this indifference may only be in relation
to what is transient. These architectural frames can
embody something more essential behind appearances,
something more fundamental and enduring. They can
place or position us in a profound relation to the world
in which we live.

This is, in a sense, the idea of the sublime that began in
the eighteenth century, articled by Edmund Burke: the
absorbing and overwhelming power of the natural landscape and our deeply emotive and profound response:
"The passion caused by the great and sublime in nature,
when those causes operate most powerfully, is Astonishment; and astonishment is that state of the soul....

45 Arthur Stace, wrote the word
'Eternity' in chalk on footpaths across
Sydney, 1963.

3 Edmund Burke, *A Philosophical Enquiry into the Origin of Our Ideas of the Sublime and Beautiful*, (1757) Part 2, Sect. I, Of the Passion Called the SUBLIME.

4 Arthur Malcolm Stace was an Australian soldier who subsequently became an alcoholic but later converted to Christianity. Between 1932 and his death in 1967 he wrote a single word message "Eternity" with chalk on footpaths in and around Sydney and extending to Parramatta. Imogen Eveson, *The Curious Story of Sydney's Mr Eternity*, Australian Traveller, < https://www.australiantraveller.com/nsw/sydney/story-of-sydney-mr-eternity-arthur-stace/>, 2018.

is the effect of the sublime in its highest degree; the inferior effects are admiration, reverence, and respect."[3]

When we look out over the ocean at the horizon, we experience a calming, meditative effect. We are placed in relation to the world in a way that is immediately overwhelming, emphasising our insignificance in relation to the vastness of the ocean or the stars. But at the same time, we are comforted, we are pleased to be such a small part, our egos recede and we feel momentarily connected. Uluru, in the land of the Anangu people and formed by their ancestral beings during the Dreaming, is perhaps the greatest monument in Australia. Uluru communicates this sense of the eternal, of the universal, across cultures, in a way that moves all of us, inviting us to experience something outside ourselves, a profound interconnection.

Architecture can also adjust our experience of the world and help us find our place within it. We are made aware of the conditions of our lives by constructing alternative frames within which things are set in a slightly different order. These are the critical frames through which we ultimately attempt to reconcile our place in the world.

At about the same time as Louis Kahn was writing his essay, Arthur Malcolm Stace, a former soldier and reformed alcoholic, was writing one word in chalk all over Sydney: 'Eternity'.[4] His fragile words, washed away and rewritten again and again, are etched in the memory of Sydney-siders. The word, 'Eternity' in Copperplate script, in that hand, although so intangible, became monumental. It is also the word that more than any other explains monumentality.

The spiritual element of monumentality is our desire to reach toward the eternal, to something beyond our limits and our brief moment. The social element of monumentality is our desire to connect to the other(s), to move beyond isolated self-interest, to shared representations and values. Both desires are an effort to move outside ourselves, to overcome in some way the tyranny of the ego, towards something greater than our individual being.

I close my eyes and for a moment the grind of the city and fogged up bus window disappear. I place headphones in my ears and the music begins to fill my ears and body. I open a novel of hope and loss and begin to read. Slowly a space opens for me to climb into. Freed from the environment of the bus, the uncomfortable seat, the crowd. The dreadful limits of my own existence are overcome in some way, for a moment.

Some form of interconnectedness begins to take hold. As I get off the bus I begin to see things differently; although I am still late, I am no longer rushing. I see the sky rather than the advertising. I feel the wind. I see in faces lives being lived. I am momentarily changed through the absorption of artwork through my being.

But only for a moment. The world will soon again close in and this moment will be lost.

The (de)Evolution of the Public Realm

For us, appearance—something that is being seen and heard by others as well as by ourselves—constitutes reality. Compared with the reality which comes from being seen and heard, even the greatest forces of intimate life— the passions of the heart, the thoughts of the mind, the delights of the senses—lead an uncertain, shadowy kind of existence unless and until they are transformed, deprivatized and deindividualized, as it were, into a shape to fit them for public appearance.

Hannah Arendt, *The Human Condition* (1958) [1]

1 Hannah Arendt, *The Human Condition, Part II The Public and the Private Realm, Chapter 7: The Public Realm: The Common*, p. 50, Chicago and London: The University of Chicago, 2nd ed,1998.

46 James Taylor, View towards Wangal
lands, Sydney, ca. 1819-20.

Over the course of many years, a pathway through the eucalyptus trees to the harbour's edge was formed by the Gadigal People. Perhaps this track was a trading route between the farmed grasslands and fishing areas of the waterfront. It was certainly an important spine-like pathway, true and turning with the contours.

Following European occupation and settlement of Sydney, the line of this track was transformed and embedded in what became the central street of the town. The former Gadigal track was forgotten and George Street created, named after the British King George III. George Street is now the busy north-south artery of the city. As this street gently turns near the centre of the city it opens to Martin Place, a public space thought of as the 'Civic Heart' of Sydney. Beyond the ring of public space around Circular Quay, which is framed by the Bridge and Opera House, Martin Place is the most important public space in the city. A former street now closed to traffic, it is a linear public space stretching east-west across the width and topography of the centre of the city.

The lower section of Martin Place between George Street and Pitt Street was officially opened in 1892 and named in honour of Sir James Martin, a former Chief Justice and Premier of New South Wales. At the centre of this public space is the Sydney Cenotaph; a memorial to great loss, constructed after the First World War, and the focus of ANZAC Day dawn ceremonies and remembrances. The great altar-like granite block is guarded by two bronze figures, stoic and seemingly unaffected by the surrounding trade and display of luxury commodity.

The setting for the Cenotaph is defined by an elegant series of beautiful stone buildings, preeminent among which is the General Post Office (GPO) designed by the Government Architect James Barnett and completed in 1891. At the time of construction it was, in many ways, the most important public building in Sydney; the great public Post Office open to and interconnecting everyone. It is most powerfully characterised by the generous north-facing colonnade that runs the full length of the city block, giving deep shade to the edge of Martin Place.

47 The Cenotaph, Martin Place.

2 Dr H.C. Coombs, the First Governor of the Reserve Bank, speech and press statement for the opening of the Reserve Bank of Australia, Sydney, 10 December 1964, Reserve Bank of Australia Archives. Dr Coombs prepared a 'mock speech' and press statement for the building's opening, but no official function marked the occasion. Reserve Bank of Australia, *Reflections of Martin Place*, Reserve Bank of Australia Museum, <https://museum.rba.gov.au/exhibi- tions/ reflections-of-martin-place/>, 2021.

This great public building was privatised in 1996, and is now an elegant luxury hotel, with the post office reduced to a small corner store. The colonnade is populated with white cloth tables for fine Italian dining, but there is still enough room to sit on the steps within the shade, with your sandwich and take-away coffee. There is also a small area in the colonnade seemingly reserved for the bicycle couriers' marginal micro-culture of the gig economy.

Opposite the GPO a fine series of beautiful stone buildings characterise the northern side of Martin Place. Their opening to the public place is now mediated through the shopfronts of Paspaley luxury jewellery and the elegant designer clothing of the Giorgio Armani store.

Further east, Martin Place rises to Macquarie Street, the ridge-line governmental street of Sydney, and is terminated by the Sydney Hospital. Here also is the Reserve Bank of Australia, a symbol of our finance and home to the weighty determination of government interest rates. Designed in 1959 and completed in 1964 this modernist architecture aimed to project a different set of values to the turn of the century weighty solid and imposing stone bank buildings on Martin Place. Transparency, efficiency and modernity together with the democratic accountability of our Reserve Bank seemed the new and fresh message, when the building opened:

Here, contemporary design and conceptions express our conviction that a central bank should develop with growing knowledge and a changing institutional structure and adapt its policies and techniques to the changing needs of the community within which it works.[2]

In October 2011, inspired by the Arab Spring revolutions, thousands of people in Australia and in many other cities in the world started to occupy public spaces. In Sydney, this occupation took place in this upper area of Martin Place, appropriately enough right outside the Reserve Bank of Australia. This widely publicised protest was an attempt to promote a pro-democracy, civil liberty, social justice message and to protest against corporate greed and economic inequality.

48 Police action against the Occupy protests in upper Martin Place, October 2011, The Reserve Bank of Australia is on the right.

Was it an occupation of our public space or was it a reclamation of our public space from governmental and corporate dominance?

Later that month about a hundred police officers broke up the protest, making dozens of arrests. The space was cleared of signs of inhabitation and restored for approved public uses.[3]

A year after the protesters were forcibly evicted there was another event in Martin Place filling the public open space with hundreds of beds with people encouraged to spend some time in them to 'rest-easy'. This was not a protest but an experiential marketing campaign by a major insurance and investment company. Presumably, there was a fee paid and perhaps this warrants a classification outside the prohibition on 'camping in public space' that was used by authorities for the eviction of Occupy protesters.

3 There were subsequent attempts to reestablish the occupation. There was even a motion put to the City Council to establish a permanent site for the protest. The first of several Council initiated evictions took place with the protest site being removed five times in early July 2013.

49 Lanz Priestly at his Martin Place community, 2017.

Another form of inhabitation of upper Martin Place begun in December 2016. Within the construction hoarding of a new commercial tower opposite the Reserve Bank, the homeless of the city began to gather and live in an organic kind of settlement that became 'Sydney's 24/7 Street Kitchen and Safe Space'. A highly localised homeless community emerged distributing food, blankets, clothing and most importantly creating a safe place for people to spend the night. Walking past this encampment of Martin Place each day were all manner of city workers.

Although perhaps there was some discomfort and some sense of social guilt in the glances of these passers-by, there was a sense of dignity in the eyes of those sheltering in the hoarding. Homeless no longer so home-less. This was not charity it was an authentic community, living, trading, working, and contributing to the life of our city. This part of Martin Place began to feel under their custodianship and both they and the city workers seemed happy to share it.

4 'The safety issue was driven home, two weeks after Tent City was pulled down, when one of the guys who had been arrested there, got beaten senseless in Hyde Park by a guy who used a shopping trolley to beat him' Unofficial Mayor of Martin Place Lanz Priestley

Paul Gregoire, *Promises Made, Unkept: Lanz Priestly on Martin Place Tent City Three Years On*, Sydney Criminal Lawyers, <https://www.sydneycriminallawyers.com.au/blog/promises-made-unkept-lanz-priestley-on-martin-place-tent-city-three-years-on/>, 2021.

As this sense of acceptance grew, it seemed the tolerance of the authorities diminished. The settlement was undermined by police and city social services with physical interventions and forced moves before finally being shut down in August 2017. The basis for the removal of this community was again a prohibition on camping or staying overnight in Martin Place. This great public space of our city was then again restored for approved uses and activities.

This forced eviction of a vulnerable city community we had begun to get to know felt wrong, unnecessary and shameful.[4] How can our conception of urban public space be so narrow and whose interests are served, who is the 'public' to which the space seems to belong?

Somehow between the invasive consumerism of commercial self-interest and the bureaucratic authoritarian tendency of the state we need to find an authentic public space. An inclusive space of civic liberty, tolerance and acceptance, an urban space of 'public appearance' that is not owned by state or private interest, but to which we all hold shared responsibility and custodianship.

Such a public space within our city would be open and organic in character, able to respond to the pressing needs and issues of the moment. It would be less fixed, less finished, its edges not suffering under incessant requirements for retail 'activation', but more adaptable to the needs and life of the community, it would be less determined and controlled by the state, but safe, and soft in its infrastructure and management.

According to Hannah Arendt the 'public sphere' has two interrelated dimensions. The 'space of appearance,' a space of political freedom and equality that comes from the action of citizens in concert through open communications; and the 'common world,' a shared world of human artefacts and settings which provides a backdrop of permanence and durability for our actions.

We are still searching for this inclusive public space in our city.

156

Architecture,
Time and Identity

*If we take eternity to mean not infinite temporal
duration but timelessness, then eternal life belongs to
those who live in the present.*

Ludwig Wittgenstein, *Tractatus Logico-Philosophicus*
(1922) [1]

1 Ludwig Wittgenstein; translated
by C.K. Ogden with an introduction
by Bertrand Russell, *Tractatus
Logico-Philosophicus* pg.88, London:
Routledge and Kegan Paul, 1922.

50 Westerland 2, a significant and
dynamic stellar grouping within the
Milky Way, containing some of the
hottest, brightest and massive stars.

Life and Time

We sometimes refer to architecture as 'timeless' or raise this adjective up as the ultimate 'grail like' objective of architecture to somehow escape time. But we rarely question this objective, it seems natural and intuitive, as humanity's fate is a struggle against our mortality and the ceaseless march of time. Therefore the nature of architecture must surely be to help us resist the irresistible drag of time, embody the immortal and forgive our own mortality. Timelessness must be architecture's mission.

Architecture is at the heart of humanity's attempts to physically order the world to support our idealised life, in resistance to the overriding natural slide to entropy. In accordance with the second law of thermodynamics, this essential natural process runs only in one direction, towards entropy, and is not reversible. Gradual and inevitable decay, decline, and a return to earth is the destiny for us all. Architecture is an essential ally in our fight against this inevitable law of nature, the irreversibility of natural processes, and the asymmetry between the future and the past.

Life itself is, in a sense, negentropic; it transforms things that have less order such as food into greater order, living cells, and tissue in our bodies. Social systems and communities are like this too, ordering a world contrary to its nature, bending it to suit our settlements. Architecture is a prime instrument in our reordering of the world, it is like life itself, negentropic. But perhaps tragically for us, negentropy is a temporary condition, momentary, and its resistance to time destined for defeat.

However, this should not deter the project of architecture. After all, it is how you lose, how gallant the search for the grail, how glorious the ultimate failure of our quest, that is the true source of our success. So what are the forms that architectures resistance to time can take, what are our options?

Absolute Resistance and Classical Permanence

Defiant of time in both form and material, this is the most primal and classical form of architectural resistance. Permanence through impregnable materials and everlasting form. Built upon platforms of rock and assembled in trabeated forms of classical post and lintel, in stone, concrete, or bronze, the embodiment of permanence. Bulletproof and impregnable.

From the Parthenon to the Seagram Building, perhaps this is the closest western architecture has come. Where even in decay and neglect, the ruin still holds a continuous and lasting identity, seemingly immune to times entropic insistence.

51 Mies van der Rohe and Philip
Johnson, Seagram Building, New York
City, 1958.

Acquiescence and Embrace

It is going to happen, accept it or even invite it. A temporal architecture, wistfully accepting that nothing lasts and all will be returned to nature.

Perhaps at its finest, this is a poetic architecture of the ephemeral, lightweight and fragile in conception, soft on the earth and gentle to human accommodation and touch. It is in the lightness and gentleness within the exquisite works of Richard Leplastrier.

Another form of acquiescence is the headlong rush into the embrace of time; a run at the cliff's edge. This is time accelerated by modern consumerism and the fickle of fashion fuelling replacement and refreshes well before time itself demands.

An architecture passing in its nature and intent, gladly to be replaced and updated. Chase the peak of the moment, the fifteen minutes that make it all worth it, then take it down and replace it with something fresh and new. The passing and ultimately, vacuous flux of fashion, rehashing form in thin guises of newness; we all know this form of architecture and no architect is quite immune to its corruption.

Perhaps more earnest headlong rushes towards the embrace of time's expiration take the form of genuine invention, subversion, and inversion of the order of permanence. A new ordering composition challenging the false permanence of existing paradigms, to pursue entropy head-on. The heroic avant-garde whose fateful end is premature death because its very success depends on glorious early demise.

52 Richard Leplastrier, Angophora
House, Avalon, 2013.

Constancy, Continuity and Contradiction

Perhaps the surest way for architecture to be immune to time is through constant replacement and reconstruction. Fight off the gradual decline and corrosion through the replacement of those decaying elements; a constant renewal ensuring ageless preservation. This our effort to hold tight onto our heritage, what we value and deem worthy of immortality. We are all familiar with this effort to freeze architecture in the moment, capture its essence and meaning in the fabric of its construction, a cultural identity so precious that we never want to let go, never what to forget, even if its true purpose and meaning slipped through our figures long ago, the artefact remains, its emptiness increasing the importance of preserving the shell, in all its illusionary completeness.

Herein lies the paradox of trying to hold on to time: we can only clutch at surface and appearances, holding them tight, notwithstanding the gradual leak of essence and identity that are entirely lost almost without us realising it.

It is this paradox of identity that is at the heart of one of the oldest thought experiments in western philosophy, the Ship of Theseus. The ship sailed by the Greek hero Theseus was long preserved in the harbour, as befits such a great cultural artefact. As time passed the wooden planks and masts that decayed and rotted were replaced with new ones until eventually every part had been replaced. Is it still the same ship? If your answer is yes, then imagine each of the rotted parts was actually stored in a warehouse until we developed the technology to cure them of the rot, then reassembled again into a complete 'ship'. Which now is the real ship, the reconstruction in the harbour or the reassembly in the warehouse?

It is hard to answer this question because although we think of identity as fixed and solid, it is really soft and subject to constant change. Identity is subject to spatio-temporal continuity. As our constructions move through time and space, as we inhabit them with the events of our lives, they will change, decay, adapt, responding to, and with us.

53 Left: Zaha Hadid Architects, The Peak Blue Slabs, Hong Kong, 1982-83.

Transformation and Adaptation

An acknowledgment of the temporal and transitional nature of identity preferences a sense of continuity rather than permanence. Time is perhaps bent a little rather than resisted, and immorality is achieved through generational extension. Architecture is never finished nor obsolete, but adapted and transformed, a continual cultural work of continuity.

The mark of the hand of time on our architecture, as on ourselves, is not seen as a making less, but the lines of natural transition and evolution. The weathering of our materials and surfaces is foreseen in our detailing, accommodated and steered towards patina and settlement into place.

This is the layered architecture of our cities, buildings extended and adapted by generations of architects. It is a respectful acceptance of change, rather than frozen preservation or perennial reconstruction.

It is also the alignment of our work with the inevitable movement of the natural world and the transformative flow of time, both sustainable and sustaining.

Ancient and Modern Simultaneity

The conceptualisation of architecture as transitional and transformative is not acquiescence; it is not giving up on immortality and contradicting humanities negentropic nature. It is a joining of old and new, past and future, ancient and modern, that can perhaps turn the direction of time a little or at least slow it down, and give us the time we need....

I am incapable of conceiving infinity, and yet I do not accept finity. I want this adventure that is the context of my life to go on without end.

Simone de Beauvoir, *La Vieillesse* (1970) [2]

2 Simone de Beauvoir, translated from
the French *La Vieillesse* by Patrick
O'Brian, *The Coming of Age, Part 2,
Chapter 2: 'Time, Activity, History,'*
p.412, New York: George Palmer
Putnam and John Wiley, 1970.

Bridges of Lebab

If it had been possible to build the Tower of Babel
without climbing it, it would have been permitted.

Franz Kafka, *Parables and Paradoxes* (1961) [1]

1 Franz Kafka, *Parables and Paradoxes* pg.35, New York: Schocken Books, 1961.

56 Pieter Bruegel the Elder, *The Tower of Babel*, 1563.

Tower

Come, let us build ourselves a city, with a tower that reaches to the heavens. [2]

The Biblical Tower of Babel, perhaps the first attempt to find an architecture that could scrape the sky, was constructed over 4,000 years ago in the city of Babylon, in what is now Iraq. The work of a united humanity, joined through a single Adamic language, this ambitious tower must surely be the ultimate project of architecture; to rise to the heavens, to take us to paradise, a great stairway to join God's dwelling.

It is hard to imagine a more noble project for architecture as that of humanity joined in a single mission of constructed salvation; an architecture of release and escape to lead us out of the trials, constraints and torments of our earthly constraints. The tower was a singular project of unity; a means to resist human difference, conflict and fragmentation. Such a noble project of unity and singularity was sure to be blessed.

But what form the architecture and construction for this great project of cohesion and technical ambition?

The Tower of Babel has understandably been a source of fascination for many artist over the centuries, searching for the right form of this great tower to heaven. Among the most captivating and enduring are the wood panel paintings of the Dutch artist Pieter Bruegel the Elder. He painted three version of the tower of which two survive. The most revealing of form and construction is the version from 1563 now at the Kunsthistorisches Museum in Vienna.

In this remarkable painting the full depth of the massive architectural undertaking is revealed like a sectional perspective that lets us see into the very centre of the tower, with its many supporting layers of masonry arches, buttresses and vaults. It seems to grow almost naturally out of the rock, firm, solid and with a sure promise of endurance, as it rises in a continuous spiral form, weaving a seemingly inevitable progression through the clouds.

2 Genesis 11:4

Bruegel had visited Rome ten years before and he seems to have drawn upon and adapted the layered classical form and geometric monumentality of the Colosseum (80AD), for his depiction of the tower as a great work of engineering and classical unity of representation. Perhaps Bruegel believed the morality of this great Roman amphitheatre for spectacle, entertainment and political distraction was to be redeemed and reborn in the new tower. The central space of the amphitheatre for performance, exploitation and violence, filled and made solid, its obscene purpose negated and atoned through a foundation that would support a great rise for purely higher purpose.

Bruegel's classical structural depiction seems convincing, the architecture of this great construction founded on the rock appears strong, permanent and true, as it spirals high and confidently towards heaven.

Fall

The Lord said, "If as one people speaking the same language they have begun to do this, then nothing they plan to do will be impossible for them. Come, let us go down and confuse their language so they will not understand each other."

So the Lord scattered them from there over all the earth, and they stopped building the city. That is why it was called Babel—because there the Lord confused the language of the whole world. From there the Lord scattered them over the face of the whole earth. [3]

Notwithstanding the stability strength of construction, or its seemingly noble and worthy cause, the project failed, was destined to fall, destined to remain an unfinished project.

But apparently it was not the construction nor the architecture that failed, but our very language and comprehension that deserted us. An inability to speak infected our bodies, betrayed our grand intent and scattered our unity. Our language was corrupted, dismantled and riddled with difference.

But this was not our doing, we were focused on this singular and true project. Paradoxically it was the intervention of the very objective and grail of our project. It was our God that struck us down, made us unintelligible and our architecture ultimately mute.

Why would God to this? Why divide humanity, thwart our collective vision, decimate our language? Were we not seeking to speak truth? Why did God fear our plan?

Perhaps God was right to be a little fearful of the consequence of the unbridled power of humanity, but quoted in Genesis, God sounds all too human, spiteful, vengeful and defensive. How can this make sense, are these really the true words of God?

Perhaps there is a nuance in the Genesis translation of God's words that was lost, and we have overlooked God's subtext.

3 Genesis 11:6-9

Perhaps the problem was also our architecture and the form of this great singular tower was not the true way to heaven; not just the intent but the construction was false and misguided. Perhaps it was the architecture that should have fallen, been broken into pieces and scattered over the earth. Only then, could the pieces be carefully retrieved, reassembled and reconstructed into a different, truer form, directed towards a different, truer heaven.

4 Walter Benjamin, *The Task of the Translator,* first printed as introduction to a Baudelaire translation, 1923, in *Illuminations*, translated by Harry Zohn; ed. & intro. Hannah Arendt, pp.69-82, New York: Hardcourt Brace Jovanovich, 1968.

Translation

Confronted with our unlimited ambition and this dangerous tower project, God robbed us of our singularity and condemned us to languages of difference, dispersion and entropy. Perhaps God was not merely blinded by frenzy, fury and fear but was giving us a difficult Zen-like lesson that required us to grow and learn. We were condemned to 'babel' in order to learn how to speak again, to find a language out of difference, rather than singularity, and thereby find a way to speak difficult truths. But paradoxically, this lesson was lost in the translation of God's words.

In his seminal essay *'The Task of the Translator'* Walter Benjamin reveals this paradoxical nature of language and translation.

Fragments of a vessel which are to be glued together must match one another in the smallest details, although they need not be like one another. In the same way a translation, instead of resembling the meaning of the original, must lovingly and in detail incorporate the original's mode of signification, thus making both the original and the translation recognisable as fragments of a greater language, just as fragments are part of a vessel.

…in every one of them as a whole, one and the same thing is meant. Yet this one thing is achievable not by any single language but only by the totality of their intentions supplementing one another: the pure language.[4]

We can only speak again through an inclusive, 'pure language' of differences. Likewise, our architecture and form must be reassembled and reconstructed from difference. The forced forms of universalisation, of the classical Tower of Babel, were fatally flawed.

The very reach towards the heavens through the uncompromising form of the tower, away from the earth, was flawed and misdirected. This was not the way to the heaven we seek.

But our mistake is understandable, the tower form is alluring, beautiful and beguiling. Its singularity, insolence and perfection are hard to resist.

57 SOM, Burj Khalifa, Dubai, United
Arab Emirates, 2010.

It seems so simple and to hold so much promise to draw us up and away from earthy complexity. It is understandable that we should have tried again, that we thought the problem was merely one of scale and technique.

Once we had realised a universal technical language of scientific intercommunication, together with a global system of coordinated economic development, then understandably, we thought we had finally made it. Finally no more babel, and lots more towers.

We loved these towers and we all wanted one, the newest and preferably the shiniest available. We love the visual purity, the simplified perfection, the ambition and arrogance of these towers; even while they negate all that is around them, deny us access and cast their long dark shadows over our city.

Tsz Wan Shan Estate, Hong Kong,
1960-73.

We thought we had overcome God's harsh intervention through the singularity of a scientific language of
modernity, with its endless invention and achievement
of the impossible. But again we failed, misunderstood
or just missed. Our towers and their making had indeed
poked holes in the sky, but with dire consequences.
This time the earth itself spoke for God, rebelled and
released its anger, while our own social unity, forged
through modern universality left us disorientated, isolated and empty. Our hasty translation of God's words
left us empowered and able to speak one language, but
also left us alone, disconnected and unable to say where
we are from and where we belong.

59 Bridges over the Ganges River in the holy city of Hardiwar, Uttara-khand, India.

Bridges

It is not through the broken classical and modernist metalanguages of oppressive, simplistic and exclusive universalisation that we will be able to speak true, nor though the singularity and exclusionary nature of the tower form.

We need to search for all the fragments of our humanity that were long ago scattered throughout the world. Find them, respect them and then re-assemble them into a new whole of fragments: A patent, tentative, transparent reassembly of a universal humanity.

Such an assembly will probably be unable to shape singular towers of misdirected perfection, but will naturally find an inverse form, a reflection. Perhaps these assemblies will not seek to join the earth to the sky, but to itself. Rather than the inevitable taper to nothing and a constant longing for more; these forms will simply connect. They will be lighter projects of literal and phenomenology interconnections that bind. They will be bridges that reconnect the scattered fragments while also preserving them, a slow project of patient restoration that still reveals the breakage.

Throughout the Hebrew Bible there is a word that occurs more than eight hundred times and that is a direct reflection of the word Babel.

60 Auckland Art Gallery Toi o Tākami, Auckland, New Zealand, 2011. A new contemporary extension to the colonial art gallery is conceived as open, tree-like forms constructed from of native Kauri, uniting natural and built landscapes into an inclusive Māori and Pākehā (European Descent) bicultural New Zealand identity.

It is the word *Lebab*, meaning 'heart'. LeBaB (בבל) has two Bets. Bet is the second word in the Hebrew alphabet after Aleph (truth), and symbolises a 'house', 'tent' or 'dwelling place'. Doubled in the word LeBaB perhaps this is a reference to the duality of the nature of human dwelling, many places in a single heart.

The heart is surely the location of our essential human commonality across all our cultures and our multiple places of dwelling, it is the nexus of life in our bodies, and the empathetic source of a true human interconnection, that can bridge any divide.

Such projects of bridging will be assemblies constructed from an acknowledgement and indeed a celebration of our difference; social, cultural and locational, but be focused on interconnection, on uncovering our essential human commonality. Such projects will be empathetic re-assemblies of fragments of differences, formed into transient, imperfect, sometimes confronting and difficult, but truly beautiful bridges.

These Bridges of Lebab will be challenging, patient, slow architectural projects of socio-cultural repair and reconciliation; projects of social equity, community and public appearance; and projects that begin to repair the life of our damaged world.

Epilogue:
Virus without Vaccine

There will be no curiosity, no enjoyment of the process of life. All competing pleasures will be destroyed. But always — do not forget this, Winston — always there will be the intoxication of power, constantly increasing and constantly growing subtler. Always, at every moment, there will be the thrill of the victory, the sensation of trampling on an enemy who is helpless. If you want a picture of the future, imagine a boot stamping on a human face — forever.

George Orwell, *Nineteen Eighty-Four* (1949) [1]

We're consumers. We are by-products of a lifestyle obsession. Murder, crime, poverty, these things don't concern me. What concerns me are celebrity magazines, television with 500 channels, some guy's name on my underwear. Rogaine, Viagra, Olestra...

Chuck Palahniuk, *Fight Club* (1996) [2]

1 George Orwell, *Nineteen Eighty-Four: A Novel, Part III, Chapter III*, New York: Knopf, 1992.

2 Chuck Palahniuk, *Fight Club*, New York: W W Norton & Co Inc, 1996.

61 John Hurt as Winston Smith in
Michael Radford's film *Nineteen
Eighty-Four*, 1984.

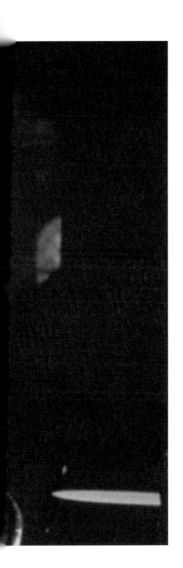

Modern human oppression has perhaps never been more dismally portrayed as in George Orwell's novel of a dystopia, which in 1949 seemed all too close, and perhaps inevitable. While it was the brutal communist totalitarianism of the east that was closest to this dystopia, the capitalist west also seemed to have an effective concentration of power through a complimentary soft and comfortable illusion of freedom and an exclusionary veil of democracy.

Perhaps more disturbing than the force of physical abuse and oppression in the novel *Nineteen Eighty-Four*, was the ceaseless control and surveillance of life and thoughts; the understanding that physical brutality was not only ultimately inefficient, but actually not enough. Communications had to be controlled to the extent that self-evident truths and facts, could be rewritten. Truth became lies and lies became truth, through the mere insistency and power of authority, irrespective of all evidence and reality. Ultimately the most important territory for occupation, were the minds of the people.

The more effective the incursions into this territory, the less the need for such crude expressions of violence and oppression, and the less visible the oppressor.

It was a blueprint for the twentieth-century social-economic organisation. Highly developed systems of propaganda became entire industries, integrated and submerged within the visible industries of culture, history, economy, and science, both in the post-war east and west.

Overt sources of coercion and manipulation were supplanted by news media, entertainment and consumption, combining to keep us placated, distracted and satisfied with a sense of democratic participation that was at best marginal or more likely irrelevant. Power, wealth and control were concentrated and maintained seemingly, through pure, concentrated, individual self-interest, requiring almost no coordination between members of the privileged ruling class.

What was driving this concentration of power and will to control and oppress humanity?

Is it the inevitable self-interest of these privileged classes irrespective of particular ideological turn, the elite, the leaders, the capitalist and revolutionaries? Is it just the inevitable consequence of a human nature that seems to compel those with any power to concentrate, consolidate and preserve it at the expense of the rest, the masses, the others, the proles?

Or perhaps, it was not just the rise of the few against the many, the rise of privilege and the exploitation of the vulnerable, but something self-destructive within in our very humanity that was released and activated at this time. We know the project of Enlightenment and modernity released great human potential, scientific knowledge, technology and power to bend nature to our wants and needs. But our release was also our estrangement; from our work, each other, our bodies and the very sense of a place in the world. Perhaps the depth of modern alienation and sense of meaninglessness within us, in a strange way, set us against ourselves, and notwithstanding the distractions of culture and consumption, a powerful agent of deep self-destruction grew. Perhaps modern humanism released something inhuman.

We have occasionally lifted from our distractions to embark on searches for those individuals we see as responsible for our oppression; uncovering, accusing and finally tearing them down, humiliating them and reaping our vengeance. But in the end, it seems to have little consequence. In any event, so hidden and integrated have these sources now become in the complexity of the twenty-first century, that it is almost impossible to identify them, in fact in some ways, sometimes, it seems to be ourselves.

We are now living in a globalised system of interconnected trade, knowledge exchange and communications. We are part of a truly global networked society with all the communication, technology and expressive freedoms that it bestows. And where has this led us?

In the advanced economies of the world, inequity has steadily increased over the last fifty years and is continuing to grow.

3 Global inequity is difficult to measure and analyse, with variation between sources including the IMF, OXFAM and UNDESA. However, consistent is the remarkable level of inequity that is increasing. According to OXFAM the twenty-two richest men have more wealth than all the women in the continent of Africa. This inequity seems deeply ingrained within the structure of a non-interventionist capitalism primarily due to the return on capital exceeding economic growth, as demonstrated by Thomas Piketty.
Clare Coffey, Patricia Espinoza Revello, Rowan Harvey, Max Lawson, Anam Parvez Butt, Kim Piaget, Diana Sarosi, Julie Thekkudan, *Time to Care: Unpaid and underpaid care work and the global inequality crisis*, Oxford: OXFAM International, January 2020. Department of Economic and Social Affairs of the United Nations Secretariat, *'World Social Report 2020,' Inequality in a rapidly changing world*, United Nations Publications, 2020.
International Monetary Fund, *The IMF and Income Inequality*, <https://www.imf.org/en/Topics/Inequality>, 2021.
Thomas Piketty; translated by Arthur Goldhammer, *Capital in the Twenty-First Century*, Cambridge, Massachusetts, London, England: The Belknap Press of Harvard University Press, 2014.

4 Don DeLillo, *Cosmopolis*, London: Picador, 2003

Worldwide there is a staggering concentration and gender inequality of wealth, our social and information communication technology is centralised and privately controlled, and we are now on the precipice of global environmental catastrophe.[3]

Unlike Winston, the protagonist in Orwell's novel, we are free to make statements of self-evident truths, but so can everyone else, about their own alternative truths. Today, the one with the most 'likes' wins; repetition, popularity and polarisation seem to be the keys to contemporary 'truths'. This is perhaps the ultimate release and diffusion of power; it is embedded within us.

But the individual oligarchs of communications technology; Amazon, Facebook, Google, Apple, Microsoft, we know who they are. Let's tear them down, put them in front of a senate committee, change some regulations, make them pay some tax, maybe even give some a suspended sentence: These people are the problem.

Perhaps one of these people might be Eric Packer, the young multi-billionaire protagonist in Don DeLillo's 2003 novel *Cosmopolis*.[4] Almost the entire novel is set within his stretch limousine, which cruises slowly through Manhattan while his money moves around the world at unimaginable speeds. The Yen stays high, losing him millions each minute. As the car moves into Times Square, Eric and his "chief of theory" Vija Kinski, are caught in a violent anti-globalisation protest. The only people not disturbed by the protest are those queuing for cheap theatre tickets; consumers steadfast to the end. On the TV screens in his bullet-proof limo, Eric watches the protest raging outside; it makes more sense on TV. The protestors are rocking the car and urinating on it, tear gas wafts through the air, as police in riot gear and protestors clash. At this moment, his theorist explains that the protesters and their violence are desirable; they are an integral and necessary part of the system they wish to destroy. The protestors are market-produced, they energise and perpetuate a total system; their actions fundamentally change nothing. In the riot, DeLillo writes, there was "a shadow of transaction" between protestors and the body politic.

62 Robert Pattinson as Eric Packer in
The Art of Making Money Scene in
Michael Radford's film *Cosmpopolis*,
2012.

Violent protest is characterised as "a form of systemic
hygiene."

Our advanced purified market system, seems to be
the greatest appropriator, recuperating all into a single
interconnected organism of control and human subju-
gation. The protestors are as much part of this organism
as the young billionaire.

Both are unimportant and inconsequential, as they are
merely part of a continuous and evolving system. The
concentrated sources of power, control, exploitation and
oppression have become entirely diffused and integrated. They are now like cells of influence and interaction.
They are all us, simple agents acting out of narrow
self-interest which contributes to the adaptation and
evolution of the whole, but are in themselves expend-
able, easily replaced by others.

This is not a mere system for the maintenance of
concentrated power and wealth, it has evolved beyond
such systemic limitations to be more like a being in
itself; a being born, within the evolution of capitalism,
from the union of hyper-consumption with advanced
technology.

5 In *Questions Concerning Technology*, Heidegger makes it clear that technology is not a merely neutral instrument but develops beyond human control and risks the way we see the world as through 'technological thinking'. Everywhere we remain unfree and chained to technology, whether we passionately affirm or deny it. But we are delivered over to it in the worst possible way when we regard it as something neutral; for this conception of it, to which today we particularly like to do homage, makes us utterly blind to the essence of technology. Martin Heidegger; translated and with an introduction by William Lovitt, *The Question Concerning Technology*, New York: Harper & Row, 1977.

Western hyper-consumption has extended human consumerism well beyond any real need or requirement, and now penetrates all areas of human life. Our entire social experience and personal identity are modified, manipulated and ultimately determined by market-driven processes of commodification and brand identification. At the same time, our technology has taken a course well beyond us, it has almost assumed a religious reverence, it will solve all our problems if we only believe and trust. But our technological is not a universal panacea, it is not even merely a neutral instrument, it conditions and distorts our relationship to everything around us, privileging human efficacy and driving an instrumental and explorative attitude to the natural world and each other.[5]

A powerful conditioning entity is created through the union of these two unlimited forces of hyper-consumption and advanced technology, that has grown so pervasive as to be a life unto its own, difficult to identify and seemingly impossible to restrain.

All forms of resistance, protest and objection are recuperated and absorbed into this life-system. All efforts to resist its influence and control will only adjust, slightly, the course of its evolution, to no real consequence, or perhaps actually, make it more hardy. It is like a virus that has long overridden our body and continues to evolve. We think we can feel it, so we claw and scratch, only to spread it more quickly. Or we think we have finally discovered the tumour and celebrate in its surgery, only to find nothing changed, it is renewed, it was only the tip of its infesting, it has no body, we were only removing our own flesh.

We have somehow created an entirely new meta-being, that consumes the essence of our humanity, while keeping us ignorant and alive.

The Internet, a global system of interconnected networks, is perhaps the first offspring of this being. The Internet has no single, centralised governance in either technological implementation or policies for access or usage. It is pure and free, unable to be controlled.

We thought it would be our saviour. We thought it would embody liberation, equality and emancipation. It could not be controlled by concentrated interests, so it would be a new form of freedom and equality. We fed it and helped it grow and it is now unstoppable, the lid well and truly off that Pandora's box.

It is a child of the virus, a parasite that feeds off all our thoughts, words, images, ideas and hopes. Indifferent to good and bad, truth and lies, both are equally sustaining for it. Tragically, this is not the equality we were hoping for.

The future for us is not the brutal shadow of totalitarianism, a boot endlessly stamping on the human face. It is an evolution far beyond mere physical violence; a seemingly comfortable oppression, more subtle and insidious, almost invisible.

We can influence the course and shape, we can push adaptation and evolution in the direction of greater equity, inclusion and wellbeing; we can soften the human stamp on the natural world, the degradation of our natural environment and the instrumental exploitation of animal life. These are true and just causes for our work and devotion. The magnitude and even hopelessness of the task should not deter the endeavour, perhaps paradoxically, the less chance of success the greater the poetic force and the more important it is to persist. But we are not in control of this (de)evolution, we have released a force that is far beyond us now.

The future for us is a virus in our minds and bodies that we can hardly feel. If we do feel something, a discomfort, a clawing and prod from the parasite, we will mistake the cause, scratch and bite for relief, but only slightly change its course. Things get better, they get worse, there is ebb and flow, but none of this affects the oppressive nature of the virus within us, which we learn to live with through ignorance and distraction.

In the province of the mind, what one believes to be true is true or becomes true, within certain limits to be found experientially and experimentally. These limits are further beliefs to be transcended. In the network's mind there are no limits.

John C. Lilly, *Programming and Metaprogramming in the Human Biocomputer: Theory and Experiments,* (1968) [6]

6 John C. Lilly, *Programming and Metaprogramming in the Human Biocomputer: Theory and Experiments*, New York: The Julian Press, Inc. Publishers, 1968.

*What if everything in the world were a
misunderstanding, what if laughter were really tears?*

Søren Kierkegard [1]

1 Søren Kierkegard; edited by Victor
Eremita, abridged, translated and
with an introduction and notes by
Alistair Hannay, *Either/Or, A Frag-
ment of Life, Part One: Containing the
Papers of A, 1 Diapsalmata,* London:
Penguin Books, 1992.

Index

Image Credits

Acknowledgements

I am very grateful for the assistance, care and attention to detail from Alicia McCarthy in the preparation of material for this publication and for her design of the book.

I am deeply indebted to Kenneth Frampton for his encouragement, insightful critique and support and also wish to acknowledge the invaluable feedback and comment on early drafts of this publication from:

Elizabeth Farrelly
James Perry
Jackie Cooper
Haig Beck

Thank you.

Prior Publication

A version of some of these thoughts have appeared earlier:

The Theory of Architecture and the Intuition of the Architect
'The Dialectic of Theory and Practice' Tectonic Form and Critical Culture, RAIA NSW Chapter Conference, Sydney NSW, June 2019.

The Face of Architecture and the Mask of the Architect
'A Note on Representation' UME 3 (Melbourne: UME, 1997): 50–51.

The Search for the Universal in the Placelessness of the Architect
'Search for the Universal,' On Monumentality (Sydney: RAIA, 2002): 8.

The Slowness of Architecture and the Speed of the Architect,
'The (im)possibility of Slowness' Published in UME 13 (Melbourne: UME, 1999): 10–13.

Architecture, Time and Identity
'Time Regained,' ArchitectureNZ 4 (Auckland: AGM, 2007): 26–30.

Richard Francis-Jones is a highly awarded practicing Australian architect. He is a graduate of Columbia University and the University of Sydney, and has taught in many schools of architecture. He is a Life Fellow of the Australian Institute of Architects, an Honorary Fellow of the American Institute of Architects and Member of the Royal Institute of British Architects. He is Design Director of fjmtarchitects.

Kenneth Frampton was born in 1930 and trained as an architect at the Architectural Association School of Architecture, London. He has taught at a number of leading institutions in the field, including the Royal College of Art in London, the ETH in Zürich, the Berlage Institute in Amsterdam, EPFL in Lausanne and the Accademia di Architettura in Mendrisio. From 1972 to 2019 he served as Ware Professor of Architecture at the Graduate School of Architecture, Planning and Preservation, Columbia University, New York. In 2018 he was awarded the Golden Lion of the Venice Biennale.